# Keeping the Drea

## The first season of AFC Telf

Mascots, captains and match officials before the first match
against North Ferriby United.

# Stuart Williams

*LONDON LEAGUE PUBLICATIONS Ltd*

# Keeping the Dream Alive
## The first season of AFC Telford United

A CIP catalogue record for this book is available from the British Library.

First published in Great Britain in August 2005 by:
London League Publications Ltd, P.O. Box 10441, London E14 8WR

ISBN:                             1-903659-22-1

Cover design by:              Stephen McCarthy Graphic Design
                                     46, Clarence Road, London N15 5BB
                                     The front cover is based on a design by James Baylis.

Layout:                           Peter Lush

Printed and bound by:       Antony Rowe Ltd
                                     Chippenham, Wiltshire, Great Britain

Proofreading:                   PerfectWord (Telford)

Photographs:                    James Baylis
                                     Rose Cottage, Lower Hall, Worfield, near Bridgnorth,
                                     Shropshire WV15 5LH

This book is dedicated to all the followers of AFC Telford United; those who are dead, those who are alive and those yet to be born.

# Foreword

When Stuart asked me to write the foreword to this book I jumped at the chance, largely for two reasons. Firstly, I have known Stuart for over 10 years and he is one of the funniest people I have ever met, I knew that the book would be a good read. Secondly, and perhaps more importantly, I have been incredibly proud to be associated in a small way with the creation of AFC Telford United.

It is not easy to explain what football means to people. In the early 1980s the anthropologist Desmond Morris wrote a book called *The Soccer Tribe* where he made the link between football and the roots of our tribal ancestry. He said, in essence, that football was about a display of our community identity and the importance of our common endeavour in whatever our role, as supporters, players, volunteers or club directors. I re-read the book a few weeks ago and I couldn't get AFC Telford United out of my head. A partnership of people from all walks of life has created a club that really belongs to our community, there is a different atmosphere at the Bucks Head these days – we all feel we have a stake in the club, it is quite literally ours. In an age when the big clubs seem to be more remote than ever from their communities we have plotted a different course – how good that feels. When I think of what has been done in such a short time it makes the hairs stand up on the back of my neck, I don't think there is any limit to what we can now achieve.

I want to congratulate Stuart on this book and thank everyone involved in AFC Telford United for letting us all live a bit of a dream over the past few months. I have always believed that by the strength of our common endeavours we achieve more than we do alone. AFC Telford United is a prime example of that, a group of ordinary people doing extraordinary things. Long may it continue.

Enjoy the book.

**David Wright MP**

# Introduction

What follows is a diary of my time with AFC Telford United over their inaugural season. It is presented exactly as I wrote it. It is my thoughts, observations and reflections of the season as it unfolded.

I hope any reader will remember that its entries were made up to nine months apart, so if I appear to be repeating myself or stating the obvious that is because I am commenting on what I am seeing at that moment. It is a diary not a novel; neither I nor anyone else could know what the next entry would be. No part of it has been amended with the benefit of hindsight.

If there are occasions when I appear to be explaining events that need no explaining it is because a diary is also the first draft of history and so should make sense to a reader many years from now.

**Stuart Williams**
**Telford, July 2005**


## Acknowledgments

I would like to thank Lee Carter, Simon Shakeshaft, Wyn Pryce, and Dave Topping for allowing me to write this book; Dave Simpson for explaining the offside rule to me, Sharon Lawley for always smiling no matter how busy she was and Ann Wellings for the tea on cold January afternoons. Thanks to Chris Hudson from the *Shropshire Star* for his support. Thanks to Peter Lush and Dave Farrar of London League Publications Ltd for having faith enough to publish my words and James Baylis whose excellent photography will make this book so much more bearable to the reader and help distract from my ramblings. Thanks also to Stephen McCarthy for designing the cover, and to the staff of Antony Rowe Ltd for printing the book. But most of all I must thank Bernard McNally, 'The Gaffer', for showing me so much patience and friendship without which this book would never have been written.

**Stuart Williams**

The opinions and views in this book are those of Stuart Williams, and are not necessarily those of AFC Telford United Ltd or London League Publications Ltd.

# About the author

Stuart Williams was born and raised in Telford. His first experience of Telford United was being taken to a civic reception for the team after they won the FA Trophy in 1970. He has been a fair-weather supporter of both Telford United and Birmingham City ever since, but 18 years as a skydiver and parachute instructor did not leave many Saturdays free. However, most people would agree that skydiving was probably less painful than following either Telford United or Birmingham City during most of the last 20 years.

After attending The University of Birmingham he qualified as a maths teacher and has written on politics, education and sport. His first book *The Secret Diary of a Teacher* was published in *Private Eye* in April 2004.

# About the photographer

James Baylis was AFC Telford United's official club photographer for their inaugural season in the Unibond Northern League Division One.

He has however, been a regular visitor to the Bucks Head stadium to photograph Telford United over the last five years.

Last season he was delighted to have his pictures published in the *Shropshire Star*, *Telford Journal* and *The Non-League Paper*.

He works locally in Wellington for Partnership Publishing. Publishers of the popular *Wellington News* and the AFC Telford United matchday programme, where he combines his profession as a graphic designer with sports photography and sports writing.

During the summer months he can be found with his camera at Orleton Park photographing Wellington Cricket Club or at Oakengates Leisure Centre covering Telford Raiders in the Rugby League Central Conference.

# How the dream began

25 March 2004: MIRAS Group, the company owned by Andy Shaw, Telford United's chairman, went into receivership. Andy Shaw resigned from Telford United. Telford United Independent Supporters Association (TUISA) started raising money that would eventually total over £50,000.

27 March 2004: Telford United played Canvey Island in the FA Trophy Semi-final. The game was made possible by volunteers.

8 April 2004: TUISA formed TUISA Business Group and started moves towards running the club.

9 May 2004: The Business Group became the steering group for supporters group.

19 May 2004: Telford United Supporters Ltd registered.

23 May 2004: Fundraising match between Telford Heroes and Hardchester United staged. Nearly 1,500 attended.

24 May 2004: TUISA wound up and funds transferred to supporters' trust.

26 May 2004: Decision that Telford United FC to be liquidated. Supporters trust launched.

3 June 2004: Lee Carter, Simon Shakeshaft and Dave Topping appointed interim directors.

7 June 2004: FA admitted AFC Telford United into Unibond Northern League Division One.

15 June 2004: Telford United FC formally liquidated.

1 July 2004: Bernard McNally appointed manager; Andy McKnight as assistant.

13 July 2004: Wyn Pryce joined and became a director.

17 July 2004: AFC Telford United's first game against Newtown: 2-2.

27 July 2004: AFC Telford United played Shrewsbury Town in final of Shropshire Senior Cup at the Gay Meadow and lost 5-1.

2 August 2004: Three-year five figure sponsorship deal with Capgemini.

5 August 2004: AFC Telford United given access to Bucks Head Stadium for 20 years after negotiations with Telford and Wrekin Council.

9 August 2004: Andy McKnight resigned as assistant manager. Neil Howarth appointed assistant manager and Sean Parrish captain.

15 August 2004: First Open Day. Over 350 season tickets sold.

21 August 2004: AFC Telford played first ever league match, 2-2 draw with North Ferriby United. 1,836 attended.

# Contents

**The football pyramid:**

The Premiership
The Championship
Football League One
Football League Two
Conference League
Conference North     Conference South
Northern Premier   Southern Premier   Isthmian Premier
**Unibond Northern League Div 1,** Southern League North & South, Isthmian Div 1
Level 3 Leagues (15 teams)
Level 4 leagues (42 teams)

# 1. July

## 6 July: Seven weeks to the start of the season

It was a pleasant summer evening. A warm wind blew from the south as a dark menacing sky built in the north. The local public school sits atop of a hill and looks down on the ancient market town of Wellington; its playing fields seems to be infested with artistic moles as hundreds of multi-coloured cones pattern the field. A lone man knelt and assembled a set of portable goalposts. In his early 40s with silver hair and a face that has seen much rain. As he stood he is surprisingly short. Confidently I called out his name "Bernard McNally?" It would be difficult to be wrong as he was the only one there. We shook hands and he was straight back to work clipping the netting to the frame of the goal.

A former Northern Ireland international, I wondered if he knows what he has let himself in for. He has a budget of less than £3,000 per week, no squad, only six players on contract, a big bag of new footballs, two sets of five-a-side goals that have never been assembled before and 14 days to the first competitive match; away to Ludlow Town in the Shropshire Senior Cup. As he staked the goalposts down the heavy clouds parted and a shaft of sunlight cast a long shadow across the pitch. I wondered if its warmth reminded him of Mexico in 1986 when he was part of a World Cup squad. As if to emphasise the distance he has travelled as a manager his mobile phone went off but stopped before he could answer it. "It's probably a couple of the lads can't find the place," he said without stopping work, "I can't call 'em back, I've got no credit." He looks at me and we both laughed, I think we are going to be friends.

Until last season Telford United was a Conference League side with aspirations to be in the Football League Division Two. They had their own Roman Abramovich in the shape of a property developer from Hednesford, Andy Shaw. He had promised the earth, built a million pound stadium, a hotel, laid a pitch that would grace Old Trafford and then ran out of money. Bankrupt, Telford United was no more. Andy Shaw disappeared, a group of lifelong supporters bought a bag of new footballs, a mobile phone, a £10 phone voucher, put their lives on hold and after a painful gestation, AFC Telford United was born.

With two weeks to the first match, Bernard had five training sessions to turn the 18 or so boys and men gathered in a knot at the top of the field into something that resembled a team. They reminded me of a mercenary army in shirts of many colours, with emblems from sides like Chesterfield and Aldershot. A few had briefly plied their trade with the super-powers such as Aston Villa, Kidderminster Harriers, Cambridge United and Shrewsbury Town, but all were available for us at the end of last season.

The new footballs started to get dirty, the boys kicked and ran. Andy McKnight, Bernard's assistant put his fingers in his mouth and blew, (they only have one whistle and it's Bernard's turn this evening) the mob halted and Andy shouted a line that I suspected I would hear many times over the next nine months "Don't cross just because you can, think about the angles." Like a chess player analysing his endgame Andy moved them all back to where they were, he pointed and pushed, then called "Play on". Again they kicked and ran, again he called them back. It's going to be a long, long season.

Two men with figures more associated with darts than football arrived on the touchline. Lee and Simon, the prime-movers behind the new club, have just been to Tesco to pick up the water for the break and after a negotiation with the bank, some credit for the mobile phone.

About 20 spectators have gathered at the edge of the training pitch. A few are wearing last year's replica shirts, they love the club with passion enough to bring them to the corner of a school playing field when dark skies threaten to watch an eclectic pack of 18 football also-rans train for a team seven divisions below the Premiership. A team that, no matter how hard you try to explain to them, is not the same team as last season, or is it? The parts are different, the name is different but to these old men and young boys the sum of those parts is the same.

It is impossible to understand what it is that happens when as a child you swear loyalty to a team but the instant you say the words "I support..." that is who you support, you can follow other teams, you can care about other teams, but once you have said those words "I support..." you cannot change your mind, not even if asked to by a stranger who has just saved your family from drowning or placed you under the most inhumane torture. It is like the unconditional love for a new born child, an allegiance that once given that cannot be cancelled.

Just after World War Two the government decided to build a series of new towns across the country. One was to be built around seven old towns in the county of Shropshire. It was called Telford after the civil engineer Thomas Telford who did much of his early work in the county. One of the towns it was to include was the market town of Wellington, the unofficial capital of the district, it had the biggest railway station, church, market and of course football team: Wellington Town FC or the Lillywhites as they were sometimes known.

The club was formed in 1879, and have played at the Bucks Head Ground behind the Bucks Head Pub since 1887; they changed their name to Telford United in 1969. My first memory of them was in 1970 when, like the children who were at the training session today, I was taken to watch the then heroic team arrive at a civic reception held for them after they won the FA Trophy. I was aged seven at the time and not too certain what all the fuss was about, something about scoring in the same goal as a fellow called Hurst, whoever he was.

## 8 July

Big news before I even make it to the training ground, Sean Parrish has agreed to sign for us. I can hardly contain myself. "Who?" I said to Bernard. He's played in the Football League Division Two for our neighbours Shrewsbury Town and also for Doncaster, Northampton, Chesterfield, Kidderminster... and even the old Telford United. At 32 years old he's a solid lower-league player, but to a club that didn't exist four weeks ago he could easily be David Beckham. He has made inch-and-a-half high headlines on the back page of the *Shropshire Star*, words like "coup" and 'talented midfielder' take up almost as much space as the list of his previous clubs.

The same page reported that Mark Viduka has just left Leeds United and signed for Middlesbrough for £4,500,000. This, combined with the £7,000,000 that Leeds paid for him is the same budget as Bernard has for the next 4,000 years. Sean like the rest of the squad has cost £0,000,000.

When I arrived at training they were playing a game a bit like netball; they can all only throw, catch or head the ball. It looks decidedly dangerous as they dive headlong at the ball and miss; I can feel the air being knocked out of their bodies. The commitment of these boys cannot be denied. Bernard made the area smaller, they started passing with their feet, it looked like total chaos: nearly 20 men and boys charged around an area smaller than my back garden. They stopped, they started, they stopped again, Bernard rearranged them again, they played on, he stopped them again, and they played on. Slowly, the chaos became order; there seemed to be less people in the area or are there more? I couldn't tell, but it looked different. Smaller by half than most of the hopefuls, Bernard commanded instant respect, they really seemed to be listening.

Lee arrived, he's excited. "Yeah, it's good isn't it; they look more like a team." I say to him, showing my knowledge.

"Oh yeah they do, but it's not that, I think we should have access to the ground by next week." He pants; he has walked nearly 100 yards and the Tesco bags looked heavy. It took me a few moments to take in the full enormity of what he has just said. The local authority own the freehold and had leased it to the old, now bankrupt, club, which means that Lee, Simon and the dedicated fans that have set up all of this, mostly with their own money have done so without even being certain of a pitch to play on. My admiration for them was growing all the time.

Bernard jogged over, Andy had taken over the session, he should look happy, and even I could see that they look like a bit more like a team, but he doesn't. He stood next to me and Lee, but is a million miles away, he was full of thoughts. I didn't yet know him that well, but I felt this wasn't the time to talk. I looked at all the hopefuls, listening intently to Andy; they sit in a circle like small children around a storyteller. Then I can see what Bernard is doing; some of them are going and not to Middlesbrough for £4,500,000.  Where do you go when you leave a team like this, we haven't even got a ground and only six contracted players, yet a few of these players were going to be told they were not wanted.

They were all good when they played for their school, they were all good when they played for their local side, to a man they have all tried out at big clubs and to a man they have all touched the dream of being professional footballers. Now aged 24 or 25 on a cold summer's evening, a club that only owns one mobile phone will tell them that they are not good enough.

## 10 July

The weather seemed to be conspiring against this week's training sessions, heavy black clouds roll above in an angry sky. The squad was playing a short 11-a-side match against itself; well it would if it had 22 members. Andy was the referee; Bernard shouted advice from the touchline. Simon and Lee are like children on Christmas morning as they rip at plastic packaging. To go with the mobile phone and the balls the club now has eight water bottles and a large water container. I was reluctant to spoil their fun but I had to ask "Why only eight?"

"One each for Bernard and Andy and one for each of the contracted players," Simon explained as he wrote their names on each bottle. Suddenly the sky which was now so dark the automatic security lighting had come on unleashed rain so hard the goalmouths instantly became quagmires. We all sprint for the cover of the porch. Bernard stood resolute shouting advice. The boys continued running, the rain ricocheted off them like bullets from a wall. I watched the water pound down the drainpipe and overflow from the drain. It was like the weather is daring them to quit, testing their resolve to play football. They looked like sewer-rats, their hair glued to their cheeks, their shirts transparent on their backs.

The rain eased off, the drain coughed and spluttered, small pools that have formed became puddles and slowly faded as the summer earth soaked up the deluge. The players played on as steam rose from their backs. They have seen off the weather, now there is only the bank, the local council and the small matter of not even having 11 first team players with 10 days to the first match, to contend with.

A ball curled effortlessly from the pack. It rose over the goalkeeper and dipped perfectly six inches lower than the crossbar. If only it had been four feet to the left it would have been a great goal. "That's Tolley!" Lee enthuses. Several of us looked for an explanation. "We hope he's going to sign today, he was playing for Shrewsbury last season." We seem to have picked up another one of our neighbour's former players, he had been a schoolboy player with them, aged 20 he had played only a

4

handful of matches for Shrewsbury and had spent most of his time out on loan before being 'released' when they won promotion back to the Football League after one season in the Conference. He played a far better game than many of the others; he stood out as being good. As he should; football and training have been his life since he was 12-years-old; he hasn't yet trained at night after a day in a factory, he's still young enough to dream, his setbacks have been minimal. Who knows? A couple of seasons with Telford with frequent matches building his confidence and anything is possible. I wished him luck and I didn't yet know him.

They all stopped for a break, the new water bottles were issued. I wondered if the preferential treatment will cause a schism in the camp but no one seemed to notice. The large water container had Lucozade in it; ice from a cool box is added. The drink, ice and paper-cups have all been donated by one of the watching supporters. Five seasons ago Newcastle United supporters had to go to court to fight to keep their season tickets after the ground was altered; those same fans would have brought the Lucozade and made the ice if this were their team. I wonder if the accountants who decided their seats must go would be here on wet July morning or do they think that a team name is just a brand and the fans can just go somewhere else if they don't like what they are getting.

## 14 July: Six weeks to the start of the season

The weather was kind to us this evening, the sky was blue, the breeze warm and the mood good. There was still an hour before the boys were due to arrive; I met Bernard as he was walking back from the field.

Lowering himself to the low kerb of the car park Bernard opened a catalogue. "We need some goals," he said to me, explaining what he was looking for. I resist making a crack about needing goal-scorers, defenders and mid-fielders to help score them. "A good set on wheels is about £400, oh well, never mind." He told me that tonight is to be about goal scoring and finishing, apparently he couldn't do this session before because he hadn't got a goalkeeper, but there is one coming on trial this evening. I suppose there's no rush as we have all of nine days to the first match competitive match. Andy was quite enthusiastic about him but couldn't remember his name; he had just been released by Kidderminster Harriers, and has about 250 league games behind him.

Bernard started his playing career with our main rivals Shrewsbury Town in the days when they punched above their weight and were in the old Second Division. Later he moved to the Black Country to play for West Bromwich Albion and by dint of having a father born just outside Belfast won eight caps for Northern Ireland. The sun and possibly the relief of finding a goalkeeper who can catch helped him relax. He doesn't like talking about himself, a trait not shared by many footballers, and with a bit of pushing talked about when he was at Shrewsbury Town and they

AFC Telford United at the beginning of the season: Back (left to right):
Brin May (physio), Gareth Jennings, Alfie Carter, Mark Briggs, Dion Scott,
Charlie McKay, Andreas Kattos, Byron Benton, Derek Wellings (kit manager).
Middle (left to right): Dean Craven, Luke McNally, Glenn Tolley, Aaron Lloyd, Andy
Pryce, Stuart Brock, Tom Griffin, Ben Willetts, Matt Johnson, Tony Lacey (fan).
Front (left to right): Neil Howarth (assistant manager), Mick Tranter (director),
Wyn Pryce (vice chairman), Bernard McNally (manager), Lee Carter (chairman),
David Topping (director), Simon Shakeshaft (director),
Sean Parrish (captain, community officer).

Pre-season action: Neil Howarth beats his Newtown opponent to win the ball.

Luke McNally makes a break with the ball against Shrewsbury Town at the
Gay Meadow in the Staffordshire Senior Cup Final.

Andreas Kattos defending against Mike Wilde of TNS

7

played the likes of Newcastle, Leeds United and Birmingham City. Though as a Blues supporter I was at a loss to understand why he put them in the same list as the other two. I pulled up a sandbag and we set the light swinging as Bernard slips into the story of the best pass he ever made; it was at St James' Park against Newcastle, he sidestepped Chris Waddle and chipped the ball to the edge of the six yard box for it to be headed straight home. Five seconds and one kick of a ball out of a career that played hundreds of hours of football and made thousands of passes, yet branded on his consciousness and relived in the private silence of early morning, or in a slow moving queue of traffic or if asked by a new audience who have never heard the story before.

The lads started to arrive, there was a lot less of them than before. They started a warm-up game throwing and heading the ball. It looked like Gallic Football, but with less rules and more danger. Andy joined in. They were all laughing but using names instead of "Ah you." The game developed a shape but still seemed no less dangerous. Somewhere in the middle of all the chaos they were starting to resemble a team - I think?

Another pack of water bottles had been purchased, so at the break there is no discrimination but tonight there was no Lucozade. The warm sun had brought out a lot of the die-hard fans to watch the training as the squad - I now felt that it was safe to use that word - drunk from their own water bottles. Andy talked about angles and protecting the ball, some of the youngsters on the sidelines started tentatively kicking a practice ball and inching out onto the pitch. One, as he passed the ball to Bernard, announced that he was going to play for Telford one day "because they are the best".

I wonder how many seven-year-olds this week have watched training at Manchester United's training ground, and passed to Alex Ferguson?

## 17 July

2-2 draw in a friendly away to Newtown.

## 20 July: Four weeks to start of season

Tuesday evening. Two days to go to the first competitive match and guess what: it's raining. Bernard was arranging his cones in a precise pattern. "This is the diamond I want to play, We kept losing our shape the other day," he told me.

Just like Liverpool who today signed Djibril Cisse for £14,000,000, we have our own foreign contingent: Andreas Kattos, a Cypriot, 22-years-old who cost exactly £14,000,000 less than Cissé. Bernard enthused about the skill the team showed; how they looked like as team and played proper football. His benchmark was Crewe Alexandra. He said that they play good football and sell players to league clubs for amounts like

£100,000. He talked seriously that Telford will do the same one day and I thought Crewe was only famous for being a railway junction.

The heavy rain turned to drenching drizzle and was sweeping across the playing fields in walls of water driven by a cold northerly wind. We stood in the lea of the building with 10 minutes to go before the training session and so far there were four players out on the field. The blueness of their calves made the words 'doing a warm up' seem like a lie. You got the feeling that these boys would crawl naked over broken glass to be 'signed' by a football team.

Bernard's mobile kept ringing. Each time it was the same conversation. The squad will mostly be late, they were caught in traffic, until now they have nearly all been professional players and arriving for training after a day at work was not an issue, suddenly it is now.

Driving for an hour after a day moving boxes in a warehouse probably wasn't on their career plan when, aged 14, they signed for 'Soso United' from 'Nowhere Town'. The match on Thursday evening is away with a 40-minute coach ride to get there, this could be a problem. Today's *Daily Telegraph* reported that the new car of choice among footballers has changed from Ferrari to Bentley. I am sure that the four lads arriving in the 10 year-old-Ford Escort will be very glad to know that their less ostentatious tastes are being mirrored by their peers in the Premier League.

Braving the elements, we all walked out to the small pile of equipment. Bernard gathered his followers around and started talking about diamonds and flat backs. Andy started to arrange flags and cones for his warm up game. Bernard changed his topic to communication. "You can't work as a team if you don't talk, you've got to tell the others what you're doing," he said and pointed behind himself to the cones he laid out earlier and started directing the lads to stand in their places. Confused they looked at each other "Where gaffer?" a few asked. Bernard looked around. Andy had taken his cones for a slalom course.

I caught part of a conversation between Andy and Bernard: they were concerned about having a full squad for Thursday. I asked him how many players he has got. "Lots," he laughed, "you ain't gonna get a game." His laughter was hollow, he wouldn't answer my question.

I knew that the squad is less than 14 strong, with two injuries and only 48 hours to the first proper match. We still have the problem of getting all the players to the ground at the same time.

## 22 July: Away to Ludlow Town

You cannot live or work in Telford without the Wrekin imposing on your consciousness in some way. The summit, 1,300 feet above sea level, has dominated the surrounding area since the last Ice Age. They say if you can see the top the weather will be fine, if you can't it will rain. As we gathered in a knot of bodies on the stadium car park the hill is truncated by thick grey cloud. It was starting to get to the stage where playing in fine dry weather would not seem natural.

Bernard stood by the rear of the coach and counted his team. With the ones going straight to the ground we were still two short and we haven't yet got any kit. It had been washed and ironed by a volunteer but the man that was picking it up was stuck on the motorway. A car arrived with the last few players and Bernard counted again. Ben Willetts, a former England schoolboy international, now works as a spot welder and had to start work at 6am this morning so that he could finish early enough to play tonight.

We were going to one of the most beautiful parts of the county: Ludlow in the Shropshire Marches. Here the night sky is very dark and rolling hills haven't changed their profile in a million years. We are less than 90 minutes from the centre of Birmingham, but could be 1,000 miles away. There are still old-timers in some of the villages we pass through who have never been outside of the county and think of Shrewsbury as the great metropolis. Ludlow is famous for its food and the arts, there are in fact more Michelin Stars per head of population than Paris and its three-week arts festival attracts visitors from all over the world. An ancient town built around a castle intended to keep the Welsh out, it seems to be half-a-pace behind the rest of the world.

Its football ground is incongruous, a modern bar, hospitality suite and changing rooms stand between two pitches with surfaces to rival any Football League team. A clue to the team's affluence can be found in the ground's name: the Coors Stadium, though why one of the largest beer producers in America sponsors a team over 100 places below the Premiership with an average weekly gate of 50, no one could tell me.

The first problem of the night was solved as the kit arrived by car, as did another five players. We all sat in the changing room in silence; no one had brought any music with them. They all started to change with the smell of Vaseline lying heavily in the air. One of them worked out that with only four teams in the County Cup competition, this is a semi-final. Not too much pressure for the first competitive match, after all they had been together as a squad for nearly four weeks and only two of the starting 11 joined this week. Andreas, the Cypriot, who joined on Tuesday, asked about the routing for corners "We're doing them next week." Bernard laughed. "Try and kick it in the net," Andy added.

Forty minutes before the match at least 200 Telford fans were lining the rail by the dugouts. Michael Jackson's *Thriller* was being destroyed by the sound system and the rain was stopping. The squad was warming up on the field; their kit looked so new it seemed a shame to get it dirty. I recognised many of the supporters from the training field; the players, running in an almost circle, were mostly unknown to them one month ago and now will hold their dreams in their hands for the next nine months.

The whistle blew and they were away. Now there were over 300 travelling supporters, we out-numbered the Ludlow fans by five to one. Straight away they all slipped into their second favourite hobby after supporting Telford: criticising the team. At this level of football the sound of the mumbled scrutiny is more defining than the singing. A player is often standing less then six feet from rail and can hear every word and some of them are not kind. Supporters who travel to follow a team like Telford on a cold, wet night like this one are not the prawn-cocktail brigade. The diamond that Bernard talked about on Tuesday looks distinctly rough cut as the team started to kick and run. Andy shouted from the dugout, some shape came back, but again was quickly lost. Ludlow had the upper hand and were like the proverbial rash for the first 15 minutes – all over Telford. "Deano' look behind you, behind you," Bernard shouts at Ben. "Get your arse back down the field." Slowly a shape developed, very slowly. The whole match had 1-0 written all over it and probably to Ludlow.

Ludlow pressed hard and Stuart Brock (unbelievably known as Brockie) jumped for the ball alongside a Ludlow attacker. His knee accidentally caught him in the small of the back, as he punched the ball away and by a second piece of dammed bad luck landed, studs first, on the Ludlow man now gasping for breath and not knowing whether to hold his back or his leg. The ref blew, the sponge man ran on, the two old-timers to my left call him a bloody poof and the two small boys to my right started singing "Let him die, let him die, let him die."

The break came and the look on Andy's face told me not to even ask about going into the changing room. Michael Jackson screeched out again. They were supposed to be playing a passing game. They were: exactly three passes every time we had possession and then a fourth to a Ludlow player. The second half looked more promising, Telford seemed to have a plan, but Ludlow scoring after about five minutes probably wasn't part of it. But we did put together five passes before giving the ball away, it was just unfortunate that this was in our own area and they scored from it.

Then 10 minutes later Ben Willetts scored AFC Telford's first competitive goal. Ten minutes after that Alfie Carter, who had not had a great start, showed some great skill as he controlled a low level cross and scored.

With 15 minutes left, Bernard used his three substitutions and brings on Ryan McKnight. He is Andy's son, tall and gangly, he doesn't at first sight look like a footballer, but with five minutes to go, jumped to meet a cross and headed the ball down at goal. It bounced short and cleared the goalkeeper.

Bernard McNally and Andy McKnight.

Neil Howarth meets an ex-Telford United team-mate Stuart Whitehead at Gay Meadow before the two sides met in the final of the Shropshire Senior Cup. Shrewsbury won 5-1.

There were times that they didn't look like the team that Bernard kept telling me they are and right now I couldn't see anyone paying £50,000 for any of them, but there were moments when they looked like a team, which four weeks ago they were most certainly not.

## 24 July: Friendly against Bromsgrove Rovers

The kick-off was at 3pm and I felt that Bromsgrove was about a one hour drive for me. I say felt because it was at that moment I realised that I didn't know where Bromsgrove was and that I had no idea how to get there. I realise at this point that I will probably spend the next nine months going to obscure little towns dotted all over the Midlands and north of England.

Bromsgrove is twined with Gronau in Germany and I think that it is likely that no one in Gronau knows where Bromsgrove is either. Once in the town I asked directions to the ground. "Turn right at the traffic lights, but most people park on the Asda opposite," was the advice I was given. It was a bright, warm, sunny afternoon, so after all our experience in the rain I knew good weather would count against us. Bernard and the team were warming up as I stepped unchallenged into the players' area and walked into the away changing room. As usual it smelt of Vaseline and sweat, the toilet wasn't blocked but it did take two or three flushes to make it work; at least someone had brought music. There was a touch of an England friendly about it as two squads were shown, one for each half, but the goalkeeper Stuart played in both halves, probably because we've only got one keeper.

If the pitch had been my lawn I would have said that the grass could have gone another couple of days without a cut, but Bernard was convinced it was too long. Before the kick-off seemed a bit early for excuses, but he's the boss. I would have been more concerned about the slope on the pitch that made it fall about four or five feet in its length. We played uphill in the first half, it was hot, we'd played less than 48 hours before, the squad all have full-time jobs and most of them had worked that morning. I thought that they would be fit getting that much exercise, and not start puffing quite so easily.

Despite Stuart pulling off a good save in the first three minutes and Bromsgrove winning four corners in the next quarter of an hour, we did seem to have the upper hand and put together a string of six passes and then one of seven that deserved more than a throw in. No score at the break seemed about fair. Our changing room was next to the officials' room. A short, fat lad in his mid-20s stood in the doorway, his black shirt and shorts were so new they almost squeaked. I realised that he had been standing just behind me between the two managers looking very bored throughout the first-half. I suppose that being the 'fourth official' standing at the side and not playing is better than not being picked or put

14

in goal. However, during the second half the Bromsgrove manager did start to make his afternoon a bit more interesting by shouting at him every time the real ref wouldn't stop the game to let him make a substitution.

It was a bit easier for us during the second half. We were running downhill. At least that was the plan, but we seemed to spend the first 10 minutes running backwards uphill towards our own goal, then we realised that the ball goes faster downhill and stopped giving them goal kicks. After 20 minutes, we were totally in control when Alfie chipped their keeper for our first goal. I had to admit it - we were playing well. Their manager was shouting at the fat kid even louder and Bernard looked smug. Even Andy's nasal tones started to sound positive.

We started winning corners like a team full of ability, which was leaving me little to be rude about. Bernard shouted to two of our players: "Next corner, play a short one." They nod and passed the message on. One minute later we play a corner that sent the ball over their box and out for a throw in. Bernard put one foot over the low wall and shouted at Alfie: "Next corner, play a short one." The fat kid stepped forward, delighted he'd got something to do; he took one look at Andy and stepped back.

The next one was a great corner. The ball went straight into their box and we nearly scored.

With 10 minutes to go we were 1-0 up and looking good, short sharp passes and keeping the ball. Then for no reason we started making 60 yard crosses and losing the ball, and then ran the ball 30 yards before losing it. Bernard was hopping up and down, the fat kid looked hopeful, we lost the ball again. I had never heard Bernard swear; he tended to leave that to Andy. When he looked at me and mumbled "We're gonna f...ing lose." How, I couldn't see it we were 1-0 up with less then five minutes to go? Bromsgrove hadn't had a shot on goal for 20 minutes. Then, a carbon copy of Alfie's goal: 1-1. Spurred on by this, we ran all over them, we just didn't have the ball while we did it; with two minutes to go they scored again.

I went back to Asda; I didn't fancy recording what was going to be said next. Oh well, only 60 hours until we have to play a cup final against a full-time professional side who happen to be our greatest rivals.

## 27 July: Shropshire Senior Cup Final

Everyone knows the atmosphere of a local derby and everyone has a list of reasons why theirs is more competitive that the others. Glasgow Celtic versus Glasgow Rangers has the 'divide' and several hundred years of religious based violence to point to. Manchester United versus Manchester City, Aston Villa versus Birmingham City, are poor and wealthy neighbours; Newcastle United and Sunderland do have a reason, but no one from outside the north-east can be certain what it is. And then you have Shrewsbury Town versus Telford United. Shrewsbury is the county town of Shropshire and it is well known by all from Telford that anyone from Shrewsbury thinks they are better than anyone else and that they should pay homage to them simply because they have the Shirehall and a very posh boarding school. Whereas anyone from Shrewsbury will waste little time in telling you that Telford is a dirty, industrial area full of car thieves and scallywags. Some often say that they once went to Telford, but it was shut. We from Telford simply point out that Shrewsbury is so desirable that the Welsh didn't want it.

It is an irony that half of the Shrewsbury Town team played for the bankrupt Telford United last season and that many of the replica shirts in our stand had the name of Shrewsbury players on them. It is strange to hear a clear cogent argument about a player's ability: "You're s..t and you know you are," being voiced by a middle-aged man who was wearing that same player's name across his shoulder blades. But then we also had a couple of former Shrewsbury players - our manager for one. Bernard had been part of the most successful Shrewsbury team ever. There was even a family connection: Glenn Tolley's cousin Jamie was playing for them.

For 20 minutes we played good attacking, flowing, passing football, then we defended very well, then it was half-time, then we let in five goals. Alfie Carter did get one, but with 10 minutes to go five more for us seemed highly unlikely.

It was our third game in six days, and the grass was very short, the floodlights were very bright, and I'm sure being this far north in the county didn't help. The away strip was very new as well so was probably a bit stiff. But the biggest handicap was probably being four leagues and about 80 places below Shrewsbury. The Telford supporters had out-sung, out-shouted, out-chanted and out-intimidated the superior, supercilious bunch of moronic clowns that call themselves Shrewsbury Town supporters. However, as an unbiased writer this is only an opinion.

I had been trying to call Simon all day to ask about the team but he never got back to me. About 20 minutes before the game I left a message to tell him I was going in the stand, not with the team. As usual I had finished with comment about his waistline and some remark about returning messages. It was the following morning when my mobile flashed up his name. We launched straight into the positive, the first 20 minutes. We talked about for this about 20 minutes. We were proud of the team. They had not let us down and had acquitted themselves well. The clichés came faster that Shrewsbury's first three goals. Then silence, then: "My dad died yesterday afternoon."

## 31 July

3-1 loss in a friendly away to Hednesford Town.

# 2. August

### 2 August: Home (Shifnal FC) to Hummel Korea

This was a very hot summer's evening, certainly not a night to be playing football and definitely not against a super fit team of Koreans after a day at work, especially when half your team is injured and the other half are youngsters.

Afterwards Bernard told me he had been so short of players he considered playing himself, but saw sense before making a compete fool of himself. So with a few players borrowed from RAF Cosford, AFC Telford played its first international. And, you know what, we weren't bad. Not great, but not bad.

With not long to go Ryan McKnight ran onto a long ball and hit it home: 1-0. It was too warm for anyone to get too excited; sweat ran from the players as they gasped for oxygen in the thin lifeless summer air. A long ball came over the top as Jamie Baylis - photographer extraordinaire - raised his camera to snap. Too late blood poured from his nose, but no one laughed (honest).

1-0 was the way it stayed, but the look on Bernard's face told me that many of the faces who ran themselves into the ground tonight won't be staying.

### 3 August: 18 days to the start of the season

The sky was blue, the grass was green and the club without a ground now has one. The manager has a desk and the director has an office. The club finally got access to the ground a week ago.

The local council had leased it for 999 years to the old Telford United, which was now bankrupt. The chairman of the old club had given the lease to the bank against the money for the development. New stands, hotel, fitness suite, car parking and a state of the art pitch. He even bought some decent players, but it never quite worked.

Simon showed me into his office, panels were missing from the walls, exposed cables run to a fax machine, the place had the look of work-under-way, so I suppose that it matched the team, the kit, the sponsors, the advertising boards promoting the... But 12 weeks ago there was nothing, the large plastic collecting barrel and the buckets stacked in the corner decorated with faded paper notices asking you to 'Save the Bucks' showed the desperate measures the supporters had gone to trying to save the old club. Not the staff thinking of their jobs or the bank thinking of its loan, but men and women who cared about whatever it is that a football team is.

Anne Wellings swept the pavement outside the entrance; she works far more hours than she's paid for, but then she would do it for nothing;

it's not the money it's not the place, it's just whatever it is that a football team is.

Derek, Ann's husband was busy in the ground. I'm not too sure what he was doing but he was most certainly doing something. "We're going to need some volunteers this week," Derek told Simon - all the seats needed cleaning. We all looked along the bank of 2,500 seats. They do not doubt that the volunteers will come in; lawyers and labourers will for a few hours bend over side by side and do the same work for a common cause. Motivated by whatever it is that a football team is.

Simon's mobile phone rang again, it is a player, a striker that he and Bernard have been trying to sign. Simon tells him of the problem of being cup-tied. Today Michael Owen, has just signed for Real Madrid for an undisclosed sum. He didn't play in a European Cup match last Tuesday so that he wasn't cup-tied. It seems ironic that the same rules apply to Michael Owen, Liverpool and Real Madrid as they do to a former Shrewsbury Town youth player and AFC Telford.

As I walked around the ground, I remembered the old Buck Head: stands built from tin sheeting, a directors' box that resembled a bus shelter, toilets that defied description and tea sold from a caravan. But it had atmosphere and history. At the moment the stands, bars and air-conditioned hospitality suites are just a painful reminder of a man who, I thought, wanted a football team to go with his car and designer suits. I don't think he will be here next Saturday cleaning the seats.

Simon's phone rang again. I walked off around the perimeter of the pitch, in the last 10 minutes I have spent more time on it than the team have. Piles of grass clippings were heaped at even spaces along the touchline and the only blemish a small dark pile of weeds in the home end goalmouth. I remember the evening that Manchester United came here and Ryan Giggs ran down the wing I was now walking along, and the ground so full a haze of body-heat rose in front of the floodlights. As I tracked across into the box, probably the only time I ever will, I stopped by the pile of weeds. It was not weeds; it was an arrangement of flowers. A card remembers someone's dad, the flowers were still fresh brought here within hours of the funeral and I knew that the club's history is safe and will last longer than this concrete and steel monument to one man's vanity. He may have pulled down the tin sheets and leaky roof, but it takes more than a wrecking ball to pull down whatever it is that makes a football team.

**7 August**

1-0 win in a friendly away to TNS.

18

## 9 August

Andy McKnight resigned as assistant manager for personal reasons. His son Ryan had been released by Bernard the previous day, but I am sure there was no connection between the two events.

## 11 August

3-0 win in a friendly away to Market Drayton.

## 15 August: Six days to the start of the season

Open day at the New Bucks Head Ground. The team were training on the pitch for the first time. Only an hour into the day and nearly 200 people had turned up to be shown around the ground, watch the training, and wait around to have their photos taken with the squad. The shop was already running out of replica shirts.

The Olympics were gaining momentum in Athens and Great Britain has won a bronze medal for synchronised diving. I have to admit I didn't know that there was such a sport. The Premiership has started this weekend and later today Chelsea will play Manchester United, whoever they are. But to the fans 'streaming through the gates', well more dribbling through the fire door wedged open with a chair. This place is their theatre of dreams.

The visitors were taken around in large groups, the guide points to the seats - where people will sit, the scoreboard - that should be working in a few weeks, the stand - where people will stand and the pitch - where the team will play. I suppose to be truthful there wasn't a lot to see, but then that didn't really matter.

The squad finished its training session and jogged to the changing rooms; the group being shown around clapped them off the pitch. I wondered what they will do when the win a match if they get applause for training.

An hour later and another two groups are being given the tour, nearly 400 men, women and children had visited so far, the shop is out of everything and the team were posing with the fans for photos, some were paying for posed pictures with chosen players. This football team is real, you can touch them, you can talk to them and you can aspire to be one of them. Nearly half of the country who even vaguely follow football will want Manchester United to lose today, the other half will want them to win, but even those who really care, and support Chelsea or Manchester United like those here today support Telford they will never get within 10 yards of their heroes. They might one day win a raffle to shake hands with one of them, but most know the closest they can hope to get is to

19

stand on the pavement outside the training ground and watch Bentleys with tinted glass speed past.

By the end of the afternoon over 500 people have visited the ground, the team were sitting around insulting each other and laughing, a few have had to leave to go *to work*. Someone mentions that Manchester United are 1-0 down, few care - others laugh. Bernard looked content, he knew that they look more like a team, he stood and looked at them. He knew they were up to mischief. He laughed and let them get on with it.

It is easy to forget that Bernard has been to a World Cup and played at the top end of this sport. Sometimes he seems takes modesty to the level of a martial art. I tried to ask him why he came here instead of one of the League clubs or Conference sides that were after him. He looked embarrassed that I even knew. He mumbled something about the challenge of building a team from scratch and this place being exciting. He was even more reticent to talk about being offered the job of youth coach at his old club West Bromwich Albion, a job that would probably have doubled his weekly money, reduced his hours and not have the weekly pressure. He did open up though when I talked about challenge and competition. Which is I would guess the reason why he is here, the weekly battle for three points, no amount of money can make up for the fix of the fight.

The afternoon was ending, people were drifting away, it was full-time in the Premiership and Chelsea have won. In six days AFC Telford will play North Ferriby United - I don't know where it is either - but you know that the battle will be fought with no less passion and the result be just a cherished.

## 19 August: Two days to start of the season

The last training session, most of the squad were here nearly an hour early, but the goalkeeper Stuart and Alfie still weren't. They're stuck in the traffic on the M6 and they've been at work since 8.00am. Bernard looked happy as he points at a tall man standing on the edge of the field. He had found another one time Premier League hopeful. Duane Courtney, signed for the team, on the edge of the training ground he scribbled his signature at the bottom of his contract, no press conferences and television cameras here. Just a biro and the top of the physio's ice box for a desk. Duane had just been released by Birmingham City after three years in their youth team. Being released by Arsenal is one thing, but by the team who haven't won anything important since... Well, never actually, must really hurt.

The plan for tonight was to practice a way of regrouping when they are under pressure and facing corners. Bernard tried to explain how they will kick the ball up the wing and then squeeze up, but most of it goes further over my head than a Beckham penalty. However, even I realised that it was a bit late in the day for practicing anything for the first time.

The late ones arrived and they began a game of keep-it-up, four-letter words and insults abound. Little Deano missed his first touch, he dropped to his knees and hopped frog-like around the grass, the rest laughed and called out, they started again.

It's obvious to anyone that now they are a team, still an eclectic group of footballing wannabees, but a team of footballing wannabees. Ten weeks ago most had never met and were all rivals for the places, now they will make a fool of themselves in front of each other.

It was impossible not to feel optimistic at the moment, as they ran out onto the pitch each knows his position. They sound like a team, they look like a team, but will they play like a team?

## 20 August: One day to the start of the season

The sky was blue, the grass was green and, it is a cliché to say so, but there was a real atmosphere of excitement in the ground. Volunteers stuck 'reserved' tickets on seats, others put up the advertising hoardings that had just been delivered while a few swept the stands. The electronic scoreboard flashes into life:

"Welcome to AFC Telford"

Then it went out again. The electrician walked towards it shaking his head - not a problem really, there was still nearly a whole day to go. Simon stood in the middle of the pitch; I don't think that he could believe that it was the eve of the first match.

Bernard appeared in the corner of the ground, always positive, he shouted: "I've got an office: all I need now is a desk, a chair, a telly, a video..." He can't complain, he's the one that chose having players instead of furniture.

## 21 August: Home to North Ferriby United

The day started well: the Great Britain rowing team won a gold medal at the Olympics. It was the personification of Olympic competition, winning by two centimetres over a 2,000 metres race, tears on the podium and the national anthem sung loud and proud. Could this be an omen for today?

One hour to the game and the New Bucks Head was alive, over 1,000 were already here. The Scrap Yard End vibrated to the sound of "I'm Telford till I die, I'm Telford till I die, I know I am, I'm sure I am, I'm Telford till I die." Not original, but listening to them sing, feeling the passion in their words I got the feeling they were not lying. The posy of

21

AFC chairman Lee Carter addresses the crowd before kick-off against North Ferriby United – the club's first league match.

AFC Telford's first Unibond League goal: Alfie Carter fires home the opener against North Ferriby United.

Telford manager Bernard McNally signs an autograph.

Alfie Carter (left) and Glenn Tolley (right) celebrate with Paul Moore after his goal against Chorley. Moore was later sent off.

23

flowers that I saw when I visited still lies behind the home end goalmouth perhaps the choir should be singing "I'll be Telford when I'm dead," because this man surely is.

A cheer so emotional you could almost see it bounce of the pitch sounded out as the squad came out to warm up. They jogged to the crowd and waved, 12 weeks ago few of the fans had heard of any of them, and a couple of them even played for Shrewsbury, but we all make mistakes and even ones as big as that shouldn't be held against anyone indefinitely. But now as never before, for the next nine months this mercenary army will carry the hopes and dreams of the people they now stand before.

Ten minutes to kick off nearly 2,000 men, women, children, have turned up to "Follow the Bucks". Lee Carter came out and thanked the supporters for everything they had done. Nothing he said was original, nothing they chanted back is new either, but it was all meant with sincerity. Nothing about this moving tide of people was malevolent; they were all just glad to be here.

Kick off. We started well, we passed, we moved, we passed some more, we moved, Bernard was silent and the crowd loud. It looked good then exactly according to the script 14 minutes in Alfie scored, the release of energy could have powered the ground for an hour. We celebrated the goal by standing still, the shape of the team was lost, the passing became wild and the (nearly) well rehearsed plan was forgotten. Two minutes after Alfie made AFC Telford history the cries of "Who" were made to seem cruelly ironic as the name of Botham made his own version of history. The beauty of their goal was not really appreciated by the Telford supporters although the three Ferriby supporters' who have travelled down, their bus driver and the one Ferriby man who lives in Telford did start to make some noise, but quickly realise that when outnumbered 400 to one discretion is the better part of valour. Two minutes later, all five of them were out of their seats as they scored again.

This certainly wasn't in the plan. Ten minutes into the second half 2-1 down, we started to resemble the rabble that Bernard selected from eight weeks ago. Then we just gave up, they looked nothing like the team that scared Shrewsbury Town for 20 minutes, they looked nothing like the team that beat a super fit Korean side.

Ferriby hit the upright, then they hit the bar, Stuart stood strong in goal, but looked vulnerable behind a defence that made the *Titanic* look sound. With five minutes to go he launched the ball down the field. Sean picked it up, but was brought down in the box. Alfie scored from the spot, Bernard looked impassive, turned back to the dugout and sat down. He knew we didn't deserve the draw.

The whistle blew, the fans cheered, and over the tannoy a crowd of 1,836 was announced. Twenty-four hours later as I wrote this up, I had just watched Paula Radcliffe's Olympics marathon end in tears, a truly great athlete sat on a kerbstone in the middle of a foreign city. No writer could ever pen a drama to match the pain that sport can create. It's going to be a long season.

## 24 August: Away to Eastwood Town

Sometime during the day of 24 August 2004 it must have stopped raining, but if it did that moment passed me by. We left for Eastwood late afternoon, we were a bit later than we intended because we couldn't get out of the car park, the barrier was down and the man with the key was on a tea break but it did give Deano a chance to catch the bus. A small group of fans had gathered on the car park to see us off, a small boy in a replica shirt sang "I'm Telford till I die" as the rain ran down his face. Until an hour ago the men in the back of the bus were labourers and shop workers, but right now they are heroes to one boy at least.

Some of the lads got down to some serious card playing after they had borrowed a pack of the bus driver, we thought about watching a video but no one had remembered to bring one. Slowly we all became quiet as the windscreen wipers squeaked and Shakey munched his way through a complete tube of Pringles.

Eastwood is a small town north of Nottingham, it was a mining town but isn't any more, but then nowhere is a mining town these days. Its main claim to fame is that D. H. Lawrence was born there, but whether he supported Forest, County or Eastwood is not recorded.

There is little original about thinking in football so David Beckham is known as Becks, Paul Scholes as Scholy, so I suppose that it is no surprise that Eastwood who play in Black and White Stripes are known as the Badgers and were formed in 1953, so their ground is known as Coronation Park. What was surprising though was that any team still has a pitch that seems to slope 12 feet and stands that I thought looked like they haven't been touched since the Coronation. A boy with a small ladder is stationed at each end during the match to get the balls of the roof; it has to be a small boy as the roof probably wouldn't take the weight of a big one. But since the BBC is reporting some of the wettest August days since Noah and his flood, I suppose that the slope on the ground is makes for good drainage.

We played uphill in the first half, Bernard stood in the rain shouting instructions, the wind and rain meant no one could hear him, but it didn't stop him shouting. Myself, Brin the physio and the subs sat in the dugout and huddled together for warmth. The rain lashed and team ran and ran. They played fluid passing football; we had them on the run right up to the point when we gave them a penalty. We all stood, the rain seemed very cold, Stuart Brock dived to his left, the ball went to his left as he punched it clear, and suddenly it wasn't such a bad night after all. That was until 12 minutes later when they scored and that was how it stayed. We played the best football of the night, for 20 minutes Eastwood had 11 men in their own area, but we just couldn't score. The ball boy must have thought we were having a laugh and decided to stay on the roof, but we just couldn't get the ball under the bar.

Over 200 supporters followed us to Eastwood, they stood in the rain and never stopped singing, they cheered each miss as if it were a goal. They outnumbered the Eastwood fans by two to one.

The journey home was quiet but not silent, we'd played well but lost. As we drove out of the town and the feeling came back into my feet, I think about the boy in the rain who waved us off and the 200 or so people who had come this far on a cold summer's night to watch us lose and how much of their happiness depends on this team.

## 28 August: Away to Chorley

When I was small my parents owned a grocery shop; I now realise that their cake supplies must have come from 'Up North' as they say because I used to be given a Chorley cake after they had been delivered. This is about all I knew about the town of Chorley until we played them. Just off the M61 between Blackburn and Burnley it is a town of low roofed terraced houses reminiscent of Sunday night television; it has the look of a place where you don't always lock the back door and you can't keep anything secret.

We parked on the road outside the ground and carried the kit in, the sun was shining and all was good with the world. Then I saw some of Chorley's players, legs like concrete columns and shoulders the width of the M6, behind them stood the scoreboard that would not be used today as it was the one for rugby league, the game a lot of these man mountains seem to have been raised on. Suddenly the sun didn't seem quite as warm.

The ground was old with history and the stand wooden. For the second game in a row we were playing a team who played in black-and-white, just like Eastwood with 'The Badgers'," their nickname was completely original to Chorley: 'The Magpies'. Apart from Newcastle United and Notts County that is.

I sat in the dugout and looked across the pitch, the goal areas were each about three feet higher than the rest of the pitch with a slope of about one in one on the edge of the area. An advertising hoarding read "Red Cat Inn odd at its best". I stared at it for about 10 minutes before I realised it should have said food at its best; but then we were in Lancashire.

Before kick-off over 100 Telford supporters had filled the one stand and were already singing. A flag 20 feet by 10 feet hung in the stand - AFC Telford had arrived. We outnumbered the Chorley fans by two to one. Again the love of the club had outweighed common sense. We hadn't yet won a match and today were over 200 miles from home, but still they kept coming. Andreas Kattos ran out to warm up. The fans started singing "Kattos is from Cyprus, Kattos is from Cyprus". He hasn't had the greatest of starts to his season, I know that Bernard is trying to sign another defender, yet Andreas seems popular and always gives his all. There are decisions to be made that I am glad are not down to me.

Within minutes of the off we are in charge, playing football as if it were easy. We just couldn't score even though most of the team was playing some of the best football of their lives. Then, with only a minute of the first half to go, Andreas swung his right leg with beauty and precision, right into the nose of a Chorley player. Brockie had saved a penalty in the pouring rain at Eastwood. Today he didn't, 1-0.

Sean ran out for the second half with purpose. The rest followed, whatever Bernard had said must have worked, within minutes Duane Courtney, Paul Moore and that man Dean Craven put together a series of passes that left Sean a simple tap in for 1-1. Minutes later Paul got one of his own as he hit in a rebound from Alfie Carter. Ten minutes later Paul was probably still on a high from scoring when he elbowed a Chorley player and decided that we only need 10 men. Bernard reshuffled his pack and brought on Carl Tranter who I thought proved that we did only need 10 men.

I knew as soon as we had arrived in Chorley that this was a friendly town, but now I feel that I might retire here.

As the bus headed south, it carried many contented smiles, the radio hissed with the AM signal of BBC's *Five Live* as the sports results came in, Arsenal were now 44 games unbeaten, but who cared - we were one. The excited chatter changed to deferential silence, the card game halted and I swear that every car on the M6 slowed as Kelly Holmes moved to the start line in the Olympics. As she reached the bell most of us were standing pushing closer to the radio speakers, fists were clenched, bodies twitching, as she crossed the line we cheered, we clapped, we smiled, the clenched fists now punched the air. Her triumph was ours, she had won for Britain, she had won for us. We had won one, we had won one for the fans who had spent their nights sewing a flag as big as their hearts, who had travelled in the rain to Eastwood and never stopped believing.

Telford versus Brigg Town – The Brigg keeper catches the ball ahead of Alfie Carter.

# 3. September

## 4 September: FA Cup - away to Horden Colliery Welfare

The magic of the FA Cup is that it is the place where the minnows have their day. It would be so exciting - AFC Telford's first cup match. Well it would have been exciting for me if had I been there. Months ago I had agreed to go to London with my girlfriend, when logical arguments such as "but I have to go" didn't work, I resorted to the tried and tested sulking, puffing and panting, not speaking and even suggested that I could get a train to somewhere north of Hartlepool from London and be back in time for the theatre on Saturday night. I actually believe she was enjoying the sadistic pleasure of not letting me go. As we drove down on the Friday evening I felt the beginning of the stomach ache I used to get as a child when my parents made me go with them to visit relatives on a Sunday afternoon, I would lie on the back seat of the car crying and griping myself as if I were suffering acute appendicitis. But at least they didn't make me miss the FA Cup.

I woke early Saturday morning, she lay sleeping, and completely oblivious to the misery I was feeling. The television set in the room still welcomed us by name to the hotel; I lay and planned my day. I was going to eat the biggest breakfast I could, stuff myself, then when she wanted to go for a nice little lunch about midday I would be too full and she'd have to eat alone. That would show her and then no mater how funny the show was I wouldn't laugh and the leading man wouldn't be very convincing and the leading lady would be too big for the part. After all I'm a grown man and I should be allowed to go to football if I want.

When she finally stirred I did make her a cup of tea but didn't leave the tea bag in long enough so it was a bit weak, oh yes my plan was working perfectly, then I quickly showered and dressed so I was sat waiting for her. Waving the television remote as if it were a weapon, I couldn't find *Sky Sports* so settled for *BBC News*. A gun pointed back at me out of the screen, the voice over said something about confusion over the number of dead probably more than 100, I flicked off and onto the cartoon channel.

Slowly I ate my third sausage, I felt lethargic and it was only 8.45 in the morning. Horden was so far away that the team were travelling up on the Friday night, I could have gone with them or on the supporters' bus, which was leaving in about an hour. Instead I was being taken to the land of Albert Square, well the West End, but it's all the same town. As we left the hotel it was quickly 1-0 to me she had left her purse in the room and needed to go back up for it. I stood in the foyer puffing and tutting, staring at the plasma screen of the muted television set showing smoke poured from a building and men in combat gear shot from behind parked cars, I had little interest - I should be on a bus going to an FA Cup match.

We wander aimlessly around shoe shops and clothes shops, at 1.15 it's 2-0 to me, "I'm not hungry, you have something if you want, a still water please, no ice." Much strained silence. Later I insisted on paying the bill, the pub was dark and full of people looking happy, this annoyed me even more. High above the bar another television set repeated the pictures I had seen earlier.

Outside, streets were being cordoned off for the Tour-of-England bike race; well I suppose that minority sports are alright if you're into that sort of thing.

I remember little of the afternoon other than an almost disabling pain in my side at 3.00pm that abated about 5.00pm. At least Telford had done me the favour of losing 1-0, a 5-0 win or two goals in the last three minutes to snatch a dramatic win would have been more that I could have stood. Did I really want them to lose because I wasn't there? I hope not, but I don't honestly know. The show was good, I laughed out loud, we stood and clapped, I could keep it up my sulk no longer.

Sunday morning was sunny; I made the tea properly this time, and searched for the Sunday morning repeat of *Match of the Day.* I found more news, the same pictures as yesterday, this time I listened. On the Friday when I was sulking about going to London, Russian troops had stormed the school that was under siege in Beslan; during Saturday as my sulk was growing the body count of children was climbing in parallel, at about the same time as Telford kicked off it was about 300. The image of a soldier carrying a baby in his arms, his AK47 slung over his shoulder marched at me out of the screen. As the camera cut away a small boy looked into my hotel room, his eyes asked me what my problem was. The light blue of his shirt contrasted with the lighter blue of the sky, the white of the writing on his shirt was smudged with dirt, the replica football shirt of Lazio connected me to him, him to the people who had followed AFC Telford to Horden while I had sulked, to the millions who had gone to see their team play while he had run from explosions and gunfire.

Less than a century ago Ireland fought England with guns, now we just play them at football and rugby, for the boy in the Lazio shirt let us hope that Russia and Chennai are doing the same soon.

## 7 September: Home to Colwyn Bay

Funny old game football, I'm sure that I'll think that a few more times this season, three days after losing to a much lower team in the FA Cup and seven days after only just managing as draw in the league we played a game of football so confidently and assured. We should have won 5-0, but then I would say that wouldn't I?

An hour before the match more than 1,000 supporters were in the ground, old and young, the faithful and a few new ones. Our home gates have consistently been more than 1,000 more than any other club in the league. Our travelling support has always out numbered the opposition by two to one. After Chorley and Eastwood, the Bucks Head feels like the Millennium Stadium. Well, it would if the scoreboard was working. A local under-9s team had been invited to be ball-boys for the evening and a local law firm had just become the club's lawyers. This turns out to be more prophetic than anyone could have realised. By the end of the night we had managed to kick five balls out of the ground, not the easy way over the low unfinished side, but right over the roof of the hotel. Given that the car park was full, this must have given both the ball boys and the lawyers a busy evening.

The game was fast from the kick off. We ran and Colwyn Bay ran, but we ran faster. We passed the ball like the professionals we are. It was a joy to watch. After about 20 minutes, Luke McNally passed to Alfie Carter, Alfie went past one defender and knocked the ball past two more. The crowd held its breath, Sean Parrish hit it hard and we were in front. 1,352 people all exhaled, well 1,320 as Colwyn had brought 30 fans with them and there were two people there who I suspected were Welsh, but I have no proof of that yet.

For the first time we went into half-time in the lead, for the first time I was confident we could not lose. I cannot imagine Bernard yelling at anyone, I doubt there was an Alex Fergusson hairdryer attack or any football boots kicked across the changing rooms at the end of the last match, yet today they seemed a different team. As we worked hard in the second half, Colwyn started to defend deeper. I felt sorry for Stuart who was alone in his goalmouth as the other 21 players on the pitch played at the other end.

By 80 minutes I'm on a high, we can't lose, can we? But last Saturday England gave a lead away to Austria. No, we can't lose but we're only one goal ahead. With 10 minutes to go Glenn Tolley blasted the ball at goal to put the game beyond the Celts' reach, but only hit the bar. Bernard had given up shouting advice. He stood still; only his eyes moved to follow the ball. With less than five minutes left Colwyn threatened for the only time in the match. I looked away, the noise of the crowd told me they had missed. We won, the last five minutes put a year on my age. I know that I have felt all of these emotions before; a match just as important, England versus Argentina the 2002 World Cup for the last 10 minutes, 11 Englishmen stood resolute in their own area as I sat, stood, sat and paced the floor. Tonight we fought and beat the Welsh and as the final whistle went I felt like we could beat the world.

Bernard smiles a relived smile as we walk towards the changing room "What did you say to them this week?" I asked, all he would say was that he spoke to each one individually, he wouldn't tell me what he said, but whatever it was it worked.

31

Carl Tranter in action against his former team Colwyn Bay at the Bucks Head.

A young AFC Telford fans known as 'H' helps the Horden Welfare keeper tie the
nets to the goalpost at the FA Cup match against Horden.

## 11 September: Home to Brigg Town

By the end of this season I will be a millionaire. All I've got to do is bet on Telford to win every other match. We lost last Saturday, won last Tuesday, we lost today, we won two Saturdays ago so therefore if I put my house, my life savings, and the money my mum has is a box under her bed on us to win next Saturday I will be in the money.

I don't think that I can take another nine months of this; win, lose, play well, play badly. I'm sure they are doing it deliberately. We played well but we just couldn't score. Alfie did have a couple of good shots and if they'd gone in the net they would have been goals. A minute before halftime Glenn hit a beauty from 25 yards. It was destined for the top left corner, it had an address and stamp on it, but the Brigg Town goalkeeper stopped it from reaching its destination more efficiently than a psychopathic postman with a grudge.

And so it carried on for the next 45 minutes. Nearly 1,500 people had turned up to watch and get frustrated - well apart from the 25 Brigg Town supporters. Yet standing in the crowd, consistently five times the size of any other in this League, I had the feeling that it will take a lot more than a yo-yo team to stop them from coming. And to be positive, although we weren't good, we weren't as bad as we were the last time we were bad, if you see what I mean.

## 14 September: Away to Gresley Rovers

Gresley Rovers play at the Moat Ground. By the time we left there that night I understood why it is called the Moat. Gresley is a small town on the edge of the Potteries made up of Castle Gresley and Church Gresley, two names we would get to know well over the next few hours.

The confusion started before we got anywhere near either of the Gresleys. We stopped at the service station on the M42 to pick up Alfie who seemed to have half of the team in his car. After a 10 minute wait Sean called him and with the driver had a three way conversation.

Sean "Where are you?"
Alfie "Can't find the place."
Sean "You were here last week."
Alfie "I still can't find it."
Driver "What road is he on?"
Sean "What road are you on?"
Alfie "Don't know."
Sean "He doesn't know."
Driver "Tell him to get on to the A4... has he got a pen?"
Sean "Have you got a pen?"
Alfie "I'm going to go straight to the ground."
Sean "Don't be f...ing late."

We left the services and carried on to Gresley. Al, the driver had been efficient and printed out a set of directions from the internet; Lee had got a copy of the official Unibond League directions that brought us into the town from the other side.

There is a pub on the outskirts of Gresley called the Coachman Inn. It has quiz nights on Tuesdays and Thursdays. I know this because we passed it four times in the next 30 minutes. In the end they decided to follow only one set of directions, but we had turned around so many times no one was certain whether left meant right or left meant left. We were doing a figure of eight around Castle and Church Gresley. After the driver spotted the floodlighting we abandon the directions and just headed for the lights.

The Moat Ground is the first semi-detached football ground I have ever seen. The turnstiles are attached to the side of the garage of the house next door and it is surrounded by houses on three sides. During the match a ladder appeared at the one stand and two boys climbed out of a garden and sat on the roof to watch the game. The pitch is almost flat to the halfway line then it climbs about eight feet to the goal area.

Gresley were at the top of the League, had had four red cards in five matches and they played like it. They were tough and fit, we had a game on. But we also had a ringer. Bernard had secured on loan a player from Walsall that day, Kyle Perry.

The rain held off, a cold north-wind cut across the roof tops and we played the best football of the season so far. With 10 minutes of the half to go a perfectly weighted free kick met the new boy's head – 1-0. Bernard's celebration almost took him to the centre circle.

He sent a message to the team, "Slow down, no rush, slow down." We ran like men possessed, we couldn't wait to give them the ball back, do throw-ins at speed, take free kicks quickly. "We're winning not losing, slow f...ing down," Bernard shouted. Not a difficult instruction to understand, I thought, but then these are footballers.

The second half was even tougher. Gresley came out fighting and were soon down to 10 men, but we were playing downhill this time. The half-time talk was simple: "We're winning, front men stay wide, everybody else stick it long into the corners." For the next 30 minutes Bernard stood in the dugout and shouted "Stick it in the corners." We carried on playing good football, dribbling the ball down the middle of the pitch. The dugout was only three feet from the fans. They joined in: "Stick it in the corners." Bernard laughed as the whole team seemed to take it in turns to run the ball down the centre.

With 10 minutes to go Kyle got a second and still we played like we were three behind. But we won, we played a hard team and we won.

All we had to do now was get out of the town. The Moat is on a road not quite wide enough for two cars; it was 10.40pm when we tried to leave, it was 11.10pm when we got out of the road. I never realised that part of the job description of a football club chairman is to knock on doors to find who owns the various cars in a street so that we can get the team bus out, and neither did Lee until then. But who cares, we won.

## 25 September: Home to Stocksbridge Park Steels

I bet there aren't many people who can say they spend their Saturday afternoons running around a football pitch dressed as a six feet tall deer with size 28 feet, and I bet there are even less people who can say they have run around a football pitch dressed as a six feet tall deer with a cardboard box on his head with two bananas for antlers. But that is what Lez does. His head was stolen at a charity mascot's race the previous week so he changed his identity from Benny the Buck to Benny the Box for the weekend. The frightening thing about Lez is that I think he is exactly the same when he's not dressed as a deer.

We lost 3-1, it wasn't pretty; the look on Bernard's face said it all. Lez only had half a costume and we only had half a team.

Unibond Northern League Division One 25 September 2004
(Top 13)

|     |                  | P   | Pts |
| --- | ---------------- | --- | --- |
| 1.  | Ilkeston Town    | 9   | 23  |
| 2.  | Gresley Rovers   | 9   | 20  |
| 3.  | Mossley          | 8   | 16  |
| 4.  | North Ferriby    | 9   | 16  |
| 5.  | Brigg Town       | 9   | 16  |
| 6.  | Stocksbridge PS  | 9   | 16  |
| 7.  | Kidsgrove Ath    | 8   | 15  |
| 8.  | Ossett Albion    | 8   | 13  |
| 9.  | Spalding U       | 9   | 12  |
| 10. | Willenhall Town  | 9   | 12  |
| 11. | Woodley Sports   | 6   | 11  |
| 12. | Kendal Town      | 8   | 11  |
| **13.** | **AFC Telford U** | **8** | **11** |

## 28 September: Home to Shepshed Dynamo

At exactly the same time as AFC Telford played Shepshed in the Unibond Division One at the New Bucks Head, a little known northern team, Manchester United were playing Fenerbahce in the not quite so prestigious Champions League. Manchester United were fielding their most recent signing for the first time, Wayne Rooney, bought from Everton for £28,000,000 and we were playing out most recent signing for the first time, David Arrowsmith who had cost us £0.00.

Kick off 7.45

| Time | New Bucks Head | Old Trafford |
|------|----------------|--------------|
| | Brock, Arrowsmith, Johnson, Courtney, Howarth, Parrish, Tolley, McNally, Perry. Drysdale, Moore, Griffin, Kattos, Willetts. | Carroll, Neville, Ferdinand, Silvestre, Heinze, Bellion, Djemba-djemba, Kleberson, Giggs, Van-Nistelrooy, Rooney |
| 7.45 | Kyle kicks off with a tap to Sean. | Rooney kicks off with a tap to Van-Nistelrooy. |
| 7.46 | Shepshed try a long range shot, easily saved by Stuart. Luke picks up a clearance and runs into Shepshed's box but not chance to shoot. | Rooney runs into Fenerbache box but shoots well wide. |
| 7.48 | | Neville runs onto a Giggs cross but no shot at goal. Heinze fouled, free kick to United. |
| 7.50 | Cross from Shepshed into box, easy catch for Stuart | Van-Nistelrooy turns two defenders, but shoots just wide |
| 7.53 | Shepshed come again, long clearance by Neil | Kleberson makes run down left crosses into box, Giggs jumps for header, goal, 1-0. |
| 7.55 | Shepshed shoot wide, Stuart kicks long, Shepshed get ball, great tackle by Glenn. | Fenerbahce come again, Gary Neville makes decisive tackle. |
| 8.00 | Perry makes run down left, crosses to Glenn but no room for clear shot. | Heinze to Bellion at back post but shot goes wide. |
| 8.03 | Shepshed attack, shot form outside box goes over the bar. | One two between Rooney and Van-Nistelrooy, completely turn Fenerbache, Rooney shoots to top right 2-0. |
| 8.07 | Sean makes run down the middle, cross to Kyle, Kyle square to Paul, shot deflected wide corner. | Heinze to Van-Nistelrooy shot wide. |
| 8.15 | Leon to Glenn, chipped to Kyle, headed over. | Corner to Fenerbahce, hit to top corner, goal disallowed for pushing. |
| 8.17 | Scramble in our goal mouth, ball kicked clear. | Fenerbahce take corner, long clearance to Giggs, cross to Rooney, shot to bottom left, goal 3-0. |
| 8.30 | Shepshed attack, Duane slides in for great tackle. | Heinze to Giggs, but no shot. |
| 8.45 | Move down middle from Shepshed, weak shot goes wide. | Corner to Fenerbahce, bounces in box and rolled past Carroll, 3-1. |

| | | |
|---|---|---|
| 8.50 | Throw in by Luke to Sean, Sean back to Luke fouled, free kick, Leon hits it perfectly 1-0. | Rooney shoots from 30 yards, good save from goalkeeper. |
| 8.53 | | Free kick to Man Utd. Rooney hits it over wall. 4-1 Rooney's hat trick. |
| 9.00 | Kyle takes man's legs after chase and booked. | Fletcher on for Giggs. |
| 9.05 | Free kick to AFC Telford, run into corner by Duane, who turned and crossed into box. | Corner to Fenerbahce, cleared behind. Corner to Fenerbahce, cleared down pitch. |
| 9.15 | Sean to Kyle, cross to Luke shot just wide. | Chip to Van- Nistelrooy who rounds defender and side foots into net. 5-2. |
| 9.25 | Free kick by Kyle 25 yards out, top left corner 2-0. | David Bellion makes solo run down right wing and beats the keeper to make it 6 for united and to become the youngest scorer in the Champions League |
| 9.30 | Man of the match Stuart Brock. We've only got one set of kit so we can't swap shirts. | Man Utd win, Wane Rooney swaps shirt and puts it on inside out and back to front. |

# 4. October

## 2 October: Away to Rocester

Today will be remembered for two of the most astonishing pieces of football ever witnessed on the field of play, one major and one minor. Arsenal's 48th consecutive win as with the precision of brain surgeons they took Charlton Athletic apart. The beauty of Henry's back-heel for their second goal will be become the stuff of legend. And the major football event was AFC Telford's win at Rocester. We were 3-1 down at half-time after losing an early lead; Carl Tranter came off the bench to score a hat trick as part of a 5-3 win. Also the stuff of legend, a game I shall tell my grandchildren about.

A one time mill town, Rocester sits on the edge of Staffordshire not far from Alton Towers. Its main claim to fame is that it was once an outpost of the Roman Empire which probably explains the team's nickname: The Romans.

The sun was shining, but the wind was chilly as the teams ran out. The pitch was flat and glistened under a fresh fall of rain. Nearly 300 supporters had followed us to the Hillside Ground, two stewards stood and stared in disbelief - I knew they were stewards because their armbands said so - as buses and cars disgorged over three times their normal gate.

Our fans had so far had been patient, but were starting to be a little less so as the games went on. A goal on three minutes by Leon had them singing, but three more goals from Rocester had them singing a different song. The dugout roof was made from steel sheets and echoed to the fists of angry supporters as they called for Bernard's head and on the third goal various other parts of his anatomy. The Rocester fans were strangely silent, but given that they were outnumbered five to one, silence was probably a good idea.

The dugout didn't seem a safe place to be for the break, so I followed Bernard into the changing room. His body language spoke volumes. I had never witnessed anything like it, I was terrified and I wasn't playing. The teapot was the only thing still upright when I left for the food queue. There I listened to 100 'managers' shout about what was wrong, whine about what was wrong and cry about what was wrong.

We started again and Andreas came on, three minutes later Paul Moore set one up for Kyle. Two minutes later he was substituted; the disgust on his face was obvious. Carl ran on in his place and the rest, as they say, is history. Two goals later and the crowd were singing "We're McNally till we die" and "Bernard's going up". Bored with saying how good the manager is they start taunting each other. The 100 by the dugout call to those at the goal "You only sing when you're winning." One minute into injury time Carl made it three and Bernard knew he could pay next month's mortgage.

What a pity it didn't end there. The passion of 300 Telford fans that had been take to extremes of despair and joy and fuelled by a bar open for the whole of the afternoon, took the two men in armbands by surprise, as they almost charged the fence between the tunnel and the pitch. The abuse was so thick it could have been spread on bread, it was unnecessary; it was the ugly side of the beautiful game. Some thought that a Rocester player tried to hit a Telford fan through the fence, others that he was provoked beyond reason. I do not know, I do know that for 10 seconds I saw Telford fans scream obscenities so loud I was ashamed to be one of them. It had been an afternoon of legend, but Carl's hat trick would be forgotten, Bernard's inspirational change of tactics - and vocabulary - would be forgotten, the character of the 11 heroes who never stopped running would be forgotten and only the memory of unnecessary violent acts will be remembered.

On the coach home we talked about what had happened, and talked some more about what had happened. I'm sorry Carl, we should have been talking about you; we should have been talking about a great comeback.

People will try to blame the lack of stewards, people will try to blame the alcohol, they will even try and blame the emotion of the game but there is no excuse for any of the behaviour of the Telford fans. And we won! I'm only glad we didn't lose - Rocester's club house is timber.

## 5 October: Home to Warrington Town

The night was cold and silver rain was falling, nearly 1,400 people had turned up to watch us extend an unbeaten run of two games. From the first ball we played like mad men, high on confidence, self-belief showing, running, passing, approving nods and polite applause from the crowd. What a difference to the first half last Saturday.

Just on the half hour Leon made a perfect pass to Carl who bent it like Beckham high into the corner for his fourth goal in two matches. We were flying now. The rain stopped, the crowd sang and Warrington looked beaten.

In every match a team has its moment and just after the half-time Warrington had theirs. I don't know what we had before the break, but we lost it. Warrington pushed and we let them, you could just see they were going to score. And then they did, it was a great pass and cool, cool header; Stuart never stood a chance.

Little Deano limped off, Andreas went on, Bernard looked pensive, Glenn Tolley came off, Gareth Jennings our own version of Teddy Sheringham, been there, seen it, done it, what's the big deal, came on. Kyle was playing like a man on a mission, a mission to get sent off that is.

"Gaffer, gaffer, get him to f...ing calm down," called Matty Johnson. "Calm down," shouted the gaffer. Did he calm down? No chance.

The substitutions worked. We came back, we threatened, we played, Leon got booked for sarcasm. Twenty seconds to go, the crowd is filing out; the physio is packing up drinks bottles. Kyle passes to Carl; Carl hits it low and hard. Goal - his fifth in two matches. We've won - we've drawn. The linesman flags late, 1,000 people stand and stare. Their 'keeper kicks out, the whistle goes, full time. That's football.

## 7 October: Away to Kidsgrove Athletic – FA Trophy

I wonder if Celtic or Liverpool have ever had to rearranged a match because of an 80th birthday party or a christening. Only in non-League football could this happen. Our match in the preliminary round of the non-league FA Trophy had been planned for Saturday. First the kick-off was brought forward to 1pm so that it didn't clash with the World Cup qualifying matches, but the police were worried that the clubhouse was too small for the possible overlap of supporters for our match and those going to watch the England game. As both teams were playing on the Tuesday, Simon suggested we played on Sunday, but Kidsgrove said they couldn't stage the match because the clubhouse was booked for a christening. He suggested Friday evening, but they had booked in an 80th birthday party for the evening. They couldn't do Friday afternoon because the players couldn't get time off work at that short notice. So at 7.45pm on the Thursday, exactly 48 hours after the last match, we kicked off with most of the first team squad injured from Tuesday.

The old Telford club has a long and proud history in this competition - finalists in 1969, the first year of its existence, winners in 1970, finalists again in 1988 and winners again in 1989. Nearly 200 fans made the journey to see if we could continue this tradition.

Kidsgrove's ground is at the end of a cul-de-sac, in the middle of a housing estate and has enough parking for three cars and a bike. I hope all the guests to the christening were walking. The playing surface is really good, it falls by about eight feet in the length of the pitch and is so wide it is almost square, but the grass is a lovely shade of green and very fast - especially down the slope.

Kidsgrove scored within five minutes from a poor clearance and it went downhill from there really, Stuart, normally so solid, sliced his kick straight to their striker who, almost embarrassed by the ease of it, rolled the ball into our open net. Then Luke McNally brought himself off with a pulled hamstring, this was a problem as we only had two reserves and one of them was a goalkeeper. Bernard kept smiling, but the look on his face at half-time said it all. Duane Courtney scored with a great header and Neil Howarth got a second, but as we gave Kidsgrove two more it really didn't make much difference.

Leon Drysdale and Kyle Perry compete for the ball against
Stocksbridge Park Steels.

Despite receiving a cut to the head Telford midfielder Glenn Tolley continues against Willenhall Town at the Bucks Head.

43

I know we had injuries and I know we haven't been together that long, but this was not pretty, in fact it was downright ugly. We normally go about 20 years between cup finals so I suppose we've still got about six to go until the next one. Some of the followers made their feeling clear as the strains of "What a load of rubbish," filtered through the cold October night. The bus was silent on the way home; Lee stared out of the window lost in a world of his own. I know our budget is minute compared to Football League sides, but it is double most in this division and most of the squad have league experience. I wonder how Bernard is sleeping?

## 12 October: Away to Shepshed Dynamo

Shepshed had visited the Bucks Head two weeks before this match. The main thing I remembered about them was the good humour and the irony of their fans. About 25 of them had come and kept on shouting, at 2-0 with minutes to go when it was obvious that Telford were going to win they launched into a rendition of "One man went to mow a meadow." They are what non-League football is all about. I wasn't disappointed when we got there, a plastic tractor pinned to the wall of the director's room and a feeling that they all loved the club, but didn't take it too seriously, combined to make us very welcome.

It's difficult to explain where Shepshed is; it's sort of in the centre of a triangle with Burton, Leicester and Nottingham at each corner. Shepshed Dynamo play at The Dovecote in the unfortunately named Butthole Lane.

Well over 150 Telford fans made the trip up the M42 and most of them weren't happy after the performance at Kidsgrove last Thursday. They became even more unhappy after the food bar ran out of burgers before the match even kicked off, but we had trebled their normal gate. I suppose Bernard did have one major problem solved for him, the team was easy to pick as he only had 12 fit players, well 13 really, but Sean was suspended after he decided to decorate his Christmas tree with yellow cards, but we didn't mention that.

It was cold, both sides were steaming before the off. And after 20 minutes of play they were about the only thing that was steaming. To say it was boring would be implying that something was happening to make it boring, it was dire. Shepshed had a good back four and our front two seemed invisible. At half-time the thought of another 45 minutes of this seemed not quite as much fun as a visit to my dentist and I was missing *Coronation Street*.

The brave predicted 1-0, the sensible 0-0. About 10 minutes into part two they thought they had scored. No they hadn't, it bounced off the post. Then they thought they had scored again. No they hadn't, it bounced off Stuart Brock. Then they thought they had scored and this time they had. Twenty-one players had all got in each others' way to create something that had little to do with football and more to do with pinball.

The dugout was surrounded by some not very happy Telford fans who in the mildest of terms expressed their considered opinion of Bernard and the rest of the team. I am sure that their arguments were cogent, organised and well thought through.  That they were prepared to listen to the other man's point of view and be understanding, but I'm still glad I was in the director's box.

The Shepshed fans offered to sing for us, but weren't taken up on their kind offer. Then our supporters began a debate amongst themselves, quietly and open to all points of view they discussed Bernard's future. Mostly this was a lot more entertaining than what was happening on the pitch; so entertaining in fact we never even noticed Alfie Carter or Andreas come on for the last 30 minutes. Alfie had been out with a pulled hamstring for a month. Alfie, like Andreas, has had his critics and I have to admit I have been one of them, but no one with any sense would listen to me anyway. He's tall, cool, far too good looking and Telford were suddenly different. A run down the left split their back four and a cross into the box met by Kyle Perry and gave him six goals in seven games. Two minutes later and he did it again. Straight down the middle, Kyle headed down, they stopped defending and looked at the linesman, but his flag stayed down. 2-1 to Telford and the fans were singing "Bernie Mac is bringing Telford back" Bernard turned and conducted the singing; they all laughed and went home happy.

Shepshed gave us a lovely curry and homemade jam tarts, their fans clapped Alfie off the pitch. How different to the way our own fans act sometimes. Shepshed and teams like them are the backbone of non-League football and the volunteers that run them deserve more thanks than they get.

## 16 October: Home to Clitheroe

I sat in the seats just behind the dugout. Bernard did not look happy; his arms crossed, a stony look on his face. The mutterings of the men around me were not pleasant and most of them weren't muttering they were just saying it - out loud - like they saw it, and others were even less kind.

I'd sat next to Bernard on the coach, listened to him on the training ground, I'd like to think he's my friend; I knew what he was trying to do, but sat in the cold of an October afternoon it's hard to disagree with all of what was being said. Even with my inside knowledge, I knew he would sack half the team tomorrow if he could. I knew what he was trying to build, but even with what we have we should not be losing 2-0 to a team that have only scored a half dozen times all season.

Unibond Northern League Division One 16 October 2004
(Top 10)

|  |  | P | Pts |
|---|---|---|---|
| 1. | North Ferriby | 14 | 27 |
| 2. | Ilkeston Town | 12 | 27 |
| 3. | Gresley Rovers | 12 | 25 |
| 4. | Stocksbridge PS | 13 | 25 |
| 5. | Brigg Town | 12 | 21 |
| 6. | Kidsgrove Ath | 11 | 21 |
| **7.** | **AFC Telford U** | **13** | **21** |
| 8. | Ossett Albion | 13 | 19 |
| 9. | Mossley | 11 | 19 |
| 10. | Kendal Town | 12 | 18 |

## 18 October

At home writing up the Clitheroe match I check some of my facts with the report in the local paper. As ever their reporter, Chris Hudson, is honest and accurate, but my eyes are drawn to the bottom left of the page a letter from a man I do not know - Steve Bleasby. In print are the murmurings I heard in the ground: "...It is imperative we get out of this League, this season and McNally has demonstrated he is not capable of doing this and needs to go now while we still have a chance..."

I want him to be wrong. I want him to eat his words, but right now it seems easier to remember Stocksbridge Park Steels and Kidsgrove than beating Chorley with 10 men or the double over Shepshed.

## 19 October: Home to Rocester

Rocester are bottom of the league. Telford are fifth and in our last meeting, we beat them 5-3 away. At home with over 1,000 of the faithful to cheer us on, this game should be an automatic three points. But then we seem to have a knack of losing games we should win. And last Saturday is still too close yet to be forgotten.

Thirty minutes and a great finish from Paul Moore: 1-0. Dave Andrewartha was making his debut and was determined to mark it by running like an athlete. We were battering them, but not quite finishing things off. Memories of Warrington came flooding back as time and time again it stayed stubbornly at 1-0.

It took until the hour for Mattie to find Alfie in space. A quick exchange with Paul leaves him running to the by-line as he crossed into the box just as Glenn arrived: 2-0. Still we ran at them but even when they were down to 10 players we still couldn't score.

So tomorrow morning we will still be fifth in the League, but fifth was only good enough when we were eighth, so now we are fifth we have to be third.

Bernard McNally and player-coach Neil Howarth ponder their side's next move as the Bucks go down 4-2 at Kendal Town.

### 23 October: Away to Kendal Town

A four-hour drive to the Lake District and some of the most beautiful countryside in the country; the home of Wordsworth and mint cake, big water and big hills, this was going to be a long way to go and lose.

With Stuart on loan at the dizzy heights of Hull City and Andy Pryce in goal for the first time, it was never going to be an easy day. Mattie had been at work until 10pm the night before and was asleep on the bus before we left the car park. I wonder if working in a factory and not getting home until nearly midnight is part of pre-match preparation for Premiership teams.

Kendal had a front two who seemed to have ESP and started to take us apart. Duane was the rock he always is and Andreas continued to be an enigma, sometimes solid, at other times I thought he was uncertain which way we are playing or what to do with the spherical thing when it comes to him.

Three minutes in they scored. Two minutes later Andreas rose high above the pack to meet a corner: 1-1. Then five minutes later Bernard was shouting the words I've heard a thousand times so far: "No Matty,

No!" Too late, Andy hesitated before coming, hit it hard straight at Andreas' rear. The rebound seemed to move in slow motion as it bounced through the mud into the empty net: 2-1.

Sean ran and shouted like a man possessed; he pointed and yelled in the fashion of Roy Keane, but all to no result. Kendal scored again just after the hour, 3-1 and for fun with 10 minutes to go 4-1. Sean got one which was less than he deserved: 4-2.

I was sitting in the stand, the game had been over about 20 minutes and the ground was almost empty as Bernard walked back out of the changing room and stood on the edge of the black muddy pitch. He seemed to be replying the game in his mind. "Long way to come to lose," I shouted over to him. He turned and pulled a tight smile, "Long way to come and play s--t." An unguarded honest comment from a man who never criticises his team, Glenn is a rising star and Leon will be fine when he develops, Sean is an inspiration, but there's still something missing.

## 26 October: Home to Willenhall Town – League Cup

Two Midland teams crashed out of cup competitions tonight by identical 3-1 scores: Aston Villa in the Carling Cup and AFC Telford in the Unibond League Challenge Cup. With England international Darius Vassall injured, their manager was forced to play Angel. Oh how Bernard must feel sorry for him having such a massive injury problem. After all he was able to field his first choice team with the tricky decisions such as of choosing between Mattie and Andreas to start. David O'Leary must be looking up the M6 with envy in his heart.

It would be too easy to blame Andy Pryce, he actually did quite well. The fact is we just weren't good enough and this after Kendal and Clitheroe. Who cares about the Unibond League Challenge Cup? I don't know, but I do know that there are a lot of people who care about this team winning.

## 30 October: Away to North Ferriby United

After the trip to Kendal I have to admit I wasn't looking forward to another long journey. I seem to be using this line a lot but 'this was going to be a long way to go to lose' and given that we'd lost our last two away games, and aren't doing that well at home either, losing seemed quite likely. Deano and Luke still injured, Stuart still on loan to Hull and Alfie still not fully fit didn't help matters either. But we still managed to take over 100 supporters with us.

A low mist hung over their ground, the pitch was flat, level, damp and fast. Allotments and gardens on three sides gave the place a closed in feel. As the mist lifted the Humber Bridge slowly revealed itself to us.

Clear blue sky and warm autumn sun made everything seem very clean. Today had a good feel about it.

We played 90 minutes of good football, we bounced the ball off the underside of their bar, we played hard, they played hard. We could not travel this far, play this well and lose. But we did, 1-0. We never stopped running, never lost belief, we just didn't win. What have we got to do to win? What has Bernard got to do to make us win? Today he could do no more. But just up the road at Bernard's first club, Jimmy Quinn has quit and he won promotion last season, 30 miles the other way and Gary Megson has quit and he won promotion to the Premiership twice. Twenty miles the other way and Dave Jones has gone from Wolves.

This week was a great game. We played so well. We lost, but we lost in a different way. Perhaps we are about to turn a corner – perhaps losing differently was enough to make sure Bernard doesn't go the way of Quinn, Megson et al. What he has done in six months with these players is unbelievable, but the fans want results and is losing differently enough?

## 31 October

I asked Bernard what had happened to Ben Willetts, "Just quit" he said "I didn't sack him, he just called me up and said gaffer my heart's not in it and quit."

He hadn't been having the best of seasons but how much it must have hurt him to quit. Because it's not like quitting a job he was giving up a dream. A schoolboy international, told he was good from an early age, signed by Aston Villa before he'd even left school. And what has come of those dreams to play for England, to play in the Premiership? They ended in a two minute conversation on a mobile phone. For most of us those kinds of dreams are just that, dreams, but for Ben they were almost reality he could almost reach out and touch them.

I admit I laughed every time I heard Bernard shout "Ben get your arse up the field." But I wonder if I would have been mature enough to quit or would have I hung on like a coward waiting for the decision to be made for me?

Damien Charie stabs home an injury-time winner at Ilkeston Town...

...and celebrates with the AFC fans.

# 5. November

## 6 November: Away to Ilkeston Town

We should have been playing in the FA Trophy today, but as we had managed to get knocked out in the first preliminary round, we were all on our way to Derbyshire instead. It as a pity really as the diversion of a cup run might have taken some of the pressure off. Although Christmas still seemed a long way away, there was a general feeling that if we didn't win today, it would be Christmas before we turned any corners. Playing so well at North Ferriby and losing 1-0 only seemed to make it worse, not just because it was three points lost, but because we had played our best football of the season there. This meant that we had to play that well this week and get the result.

Bernard looked relaxed. He always looks relaxed, but I'm sure there was a moment when I saw him look just a little pensive. I'm sure he knew that a result was needed today. The team was probably at the strongest it could be. Luke and Deano were back and Alfie was fit. Brockie was still on loan to Hull City, but Ian Simms, the most recent of his replacements, looked pretty good. But just to make life interesting Bernard brought in Ally Smith. He did get to meet the team an hour before the match, so he had plenty of time to work on set pieces, tactics and learn everybody's name. Nobody expected it to be a hard game, after all Ilkeston Town were only second in the league with a team full of solid professionals.

Ilkeston play at the New Manor Ground and a very nice place it is. It has a big clock built into the stand. We didn't know then that time would play such a part in the afternoon. The pace was fast and got faster as Kyle scored on the 10 minute mark and over 200 travelling supporters went mad. Not least of all because Nigel Jemson plays for Ilkeston now. And for one glorious minute everyone was asking him the score, very politely you understand. We did shut up 90 seconds later when they scored, but it was fun at the time.

For the next half hour it was great football if you were a neutral, and it wasn't bad for them when Ilkeston scored on about 40 minutes. We came out fighting in the second half, but it wasn't to be, they were a bit fitter and slowly it started to show. Then came Alfie; I sometimes think he should be called Comet not because he's fast, which he is, but because he sparkles for a moment and then disappears again. Today he sparkled and made a great cross to set up Kyle six feet in front of an open goal. Kyle the man who had scored nine goals in 10 matches, Kyle the man who put it so far over the top a seagull had to duck.

At 80 minutes we had a free kick and this time he didn't miss. At 90 minutes they announced three minutes injury time. Damien had come on just after Alfie. At 92 minutes there was a scramble in their goalmouth. The ball hit Damien or did Damien hit the ball? I don't care; we scored,

Bernard ran almost to the corner flag, the big clock showed the three minutes were up when the ball went in. Five hundred Ilkeston fingers were pointing at it. They came back and shot. Ian saved, the whistle blew and we had won. Bernard smiled. Maybe we can dream just a little bit.

## 13 November: Home to Ossett Albion

I wonder if it's possible to win a match without actually winning. Because there's no one other than a Shrewsbury fan would say that Telford lost today. It all started to go right two weeks earlier at North Ferriby when we lost 1-0, it improved last week at Ilkeston when we won with a last minute goal and it was even better this week with a 3-3 draw.

I don't think that there were any neutrals at the Bucks Head today, but if there were they got their money's worth. Words like end-to-end football, it was a great game, edge of your seat are all too easily written, but today they are all you could say.

All through the summer evenings that the hopefuls ran around the playing fields behind Wrekin College, Bernard went on (and on and on) about passing football. "Don't just kick and run," were words I heard a thousand times. So far there was little of this on display and when it was happening it was square across the pitch. "He should change his tactics," I heard the old guard of the Scrap Yard End say. "Long balls over the top," another 100 would-be managers shouted. Today they were proved wrong. It takes courage to stick with a plan when it's not working and 200 people are calling for your head, among other body parts. Bernard showed courage and today: "Bernie Mac is bringing Telford back".

On 10 minutes Neil Howarth headed home, it was a pity that the announcer and the scoreboard gave it to Kyle Perry, given the amount he has scored it was understandable; but still Neil's a nice guy and deserved a mention: 1-0. Then we did what we always do and let them score. Well, they earned a penalty with a good move, Ally Smith chopped down their attacker, but it was after a slick move that would have got a goal anyway: 1-1. Then just to make life interesting, they scored again: 2-1 down. Maybe one day we will be leading at half-time.

Sean came off just after half-time and on came Alfie. Glenn often gets overlooked, but his passes have got gradually more accurate; not quite David Beckham but he's getting there, and a cross into the box landed right on Kyle's toe for his 11th in 10 matches: 2-2.

Guess what: they scored 3-2 down. Then Glenn crossed into the box again, this time Damien Charie hit it hard for 3-3. With one minute to go Alfie ran through and crossed to Kyle, 1,400 people fell silent, Kyle beat the keeper, the goal was open; he missed. Bernard fell to his knees. The whistle went and we had drawn, but there is just a little bit of everyone there who went away feeling like they had won.

## 30 November: Home to Kidsgrove Athletic

Stuart Brock was back from being on loan to Hull, practically the whole of the first choice squad was available, the sky was clear and the temperature low. We had to win, we needed to win.

The next 90 minutes were not pretty; they would not have even looked pretty at the end of the night after four pints of beer when none of your mates were looking. At no time did we look like the team that we are, even I wasn't certain it was the same team who had lost with beauty and grace at North Ferriby or drawn a thrilling game with Ossett Albion.

The thrilling passing football that I know this team can play; well they were playing on this pitch and wearing these shirts, so I suppose it must have been this team. But today it just never happened.

The Scrap Yard End was silent, I stood to the right of the goal and watched Bernard, I watched him shout, I watched him point, I watched him bury his head in his hands, but I never watched him give up hope.

When they scored it was only the inevitable happening, when they scored again it was only making the score what it should be.

At the beginning the old man standing behind me said "We'll be in the play-offs for sure." He left with five minutes to go. And as for the play-offs, well who knows?

Unibond Northern League Division One 30 November 2004
(Top 10)

|     |                | P   | Pts |
| --- | -------------- | --- | --- |
| 1.  | Ilkeston Town  | 19  | 39  |
| 2.  | North Ferriby  | 19  | 37  |
| 3.  | Gresley Rovers | 17  | 37  |
| 4.  | Willenhall Town| 17  | 32  |
| 5.  | Ossett Albion  | 19  | 30  |
| 6.  | Stocksbridge PS| 20  | 30  |
| 7.  | Woodley Sports | 18  | 29  |
| 8.  | Kidsgrove Ath  | 18  | 28  |
| **9.**  | **AFC Telford U** | **19** | **28** |
| 10. | Kendal Town    | 16  | 27  |

53

Glenn Tolley jumps on Kyle Perry to celebrate Kyle's hat-trick at Colwyn Bay.

It's Christmas and Kyle Perry celebrates his hat-trick against Colwyn Bay.

Midfielder Roy Jordan makes his home debut.

# 6. December

## 4 December: Home to Spalding United

After Tuesday, today was one of those games that had to be won, but not just won - it had to be won convincingly. It was noticeable that gates were getting smaller. I know that the 1,200 or so is still three and four times the rest of the Unibond League Division 1, but that's 600 less than the first match and another couple of games like Tuesday will take the attendance to less than 1,000 by the new year.

The following 90 minutes were probably unique in football history. No team could have ever dominated a match as much as Telford did and not win. We were shooting for fun. Luke hit the bar, Kyle shot wide more than once, Sean missed an open goal from something less than three feet. I think Bernard saw more of the palms of his hands than the match as time after time we managed to miss. I remembered cold wet evenings at Rocester and Gresley when matches had 0-0 written all over them and I was wrong, there was no way today could be 0-0. We just never allowed for a display of goalkeeping that deserves a page of this book all to itself. I heard that Arsenal changed their keeper this weekend, Wenger was a bit concerned that his team had only taken 34 points from 16 matches. Well he could do worse than poach Spalding's keeper.

And 0-0 was the way it stayed. The only shot they had and the only real save Brockie had to make came well into added time and wasn't too difficult for him to catch. We played good football, we really should have won, but we didn't. I suppose that I should take comfort from the quality of the way we drew, but right now I just can't. Oh well, let's see what happens next.

## 11 December: Away to Colwyn Bay

Oh, how I enjoyed our trip to the seaside. Everyone from Telford has been to Rhyl at some time or other, just up the coast, but this was my first visit to Colwyn Bay and what a day it was. But I think Kyle will remember it more fondly than any of us

14th minute: A loose ball in the middle of the park; picked up and passed to Luke who makes a brilliant run and ends with an inch-perfect pass to Kyle who takes the ball in his stride, takes two more steps and shoots low and hard straight through their keeper's legs, 1-0.

24th minute: Colwyn Bay were angry. They claim Luke had fouled as he created the first goal, but I know he's too nice a lad to do that, honest. Their anger boils over and one of their players kicks Kyle when he's off the ball. The linesman flagged, the game stopped, the ref pointed at the penalty spot. Kyle stepped up: 2-0.

67th minute: Duane clears a long ball to Alfie who skins one of their players and slides the ball to Kyle. He turns the long way round leaving the defender behind and hits it high into the net: 3-0.

## 18 December 2004: Away to Spalding United

It was cold. In fact, it was very bloody cold waiting on the car park to leave. Lee was dressed all in black and Shakey had a new hairstyle for the occasion, Bernard arrived with a box of sports trivia questions that had Nigel Mansell as the reigning motor racing world champion and Sean had a comedy film about organised crime in a Welsh, yes Welsh, seaside town.

The bus driver set a blistering pace of about 30mph and, I think, had a machine to tell him where all the traffic jams and road accidents were. He must have had one of these machines because he managed to find every hold up and road accident between the Bucks Head and Spalding. Once in Spalding we did a few circuits of the town as a tribute to Ellen MacArthur sailing round the world and there were times when it seemed like she would get home before we got to the ground. After 20 minutes driving in circles Lee took charge, he spotted a man at the side of the road dressed in Spalding colours and offered him a lift to the ground. A lot of us were very grateful for this as the bus toilet was locked and no one had a key. I wonder if Alex Ferguson has similar problems?

Spalding is about 20 miles inland from the Wash in the heart of the Fens. It has a tropical forest as an attraction, which given the way the wind slices in from the North Sea there is about as likely as organised crime in a Welsh seaside town making a interesting plot for a film.

Kyle was out with a bug and Neil suspended. I believe him; he never intended to knee anyone - they just ran on to him as he was stretching in the middle of an argument. Spalding could definitely do with making a trip to Virgin Records. It is years since I've heard Duran Duran, Frankie Goes to Hollywood and Soft Cell; then the announcer named every member of the team including the physio; every member except Bernard that is.

For 20 minutes the game had 0-0 tattooed on it. Then they scored and a better goal will never be scored. It was an amazing 30 yard strike: 1-0 down our heads dropped and it looked like the tropical forest might be more entertaining than what was to come. The second half brought Spalding out fighting; they had no intention of losing; then Glenn hit a shot so hard it made a sonic boom, rattled the crossbar and bounced out. Lee stood and looked away; the sigh from around the pitch was audible across the town, but two people on the pitch thought differently: our manager and one very brave linesman. Bernard could have been sent off he ran so far from the dugout; the linesman stood resolute signalling for the ref. The two talked - the goal was given – Bernard stayed on the pitch and the linesman wasn't even Russian: 1-1.

With 10 minutes left we had a fee kick, Jack Cudworth lined it up, hit it low, the wall jumped and the ball went into the net: 2-1. They came back and back some more, but we hung on. Four minutes extra time was signalled. They were a very long four minutes, but we won.

All we had to do now was get home

Unibond Northern League Division One 18 December 2004
(Top 10)

| | | P | Pts |
|---|---|---|---|
| 1. | North Ferriby | 21 | 43 |
| 2. | Ilkeston Town | 21 | 42 |
| 3. | Gresley Rovers | 19 | 40 |
| 4. | Willenhall Town | 20 | 36 |
| **5.** | **AFC Telford U** | **22** | **35** |
| 6. | Kendal Town | 19 | 34 |
| 7. | Stocksbridge PS | 22 | 34 |
| 8. | Ossett Albion | 21 | 33 |
| 9. | Eastwood Town | 21 | 32 |
| 10. | Kidsgrove Ath | 22 | 31 |

## 27 December: Match postponed

It was the first white Christmas I could remember for many years and the thick frost on my car meant that I was not surprised when Lee called me to say the match was off. It was a surreal feeling as I sat in my girlfriend's kitchen discussing a non-league football match as the portable television showed aerial film of miles of flooded coast line. The body count seemed to be clicking up like a score counter on a 1960s pinball machine 20,000 - 25,000 - 50,000.

As the day wore on we were bombarded with images that belonged to Hollywood and a body count to the Old Testament. I could take no more by early afternoon, safe and warm in Telford I felt guilt at the ease of my life, guilt amplified as I heard of a group of doctors from London flying out to India about the same time as we would have been kicking off. So I turned over to the sports channel as the results from the League began to trickle in, but they just didn't seem to matter.

The countries affected were Muslim, Hindu and secular; Indian, African and Asian. The dead were from almost every country in the world. But in every one of those countries right now someone is kicking a ball, or a tin can, or a cardboard box and that someone is being Beckham, or Pelé or even Bobby Charlton. So perhaps by playing our football and caring about the result we are connecting with them more than we realise. And among that group of doctors from London you can almost guarantee that before this week is out and despite the sights that they will have see, one of them will have asked for the result of Chelsea versus Liverpool match and for a moment care just as much about that.

## 30 December: Away to Willenhall Town

"Seven quid? You're having a laugh. Seven quid? You're having a laugh." Well I hope that someone found it funny because well over 700 Telford supporters didn't. Yes, I know it is £8.00 for admission to the Bucks Head, but my shed is bigger than the stand at Willenhall. I just hope they put the extra gate money to good use.

Willenhall sits on the edge of Wolverhampton. It was once the biggest lock and key manufacturer in the country, now its only claim to fame is that it still makes locks - and that's about it really.

Postponed from Monday, it was a cold and clear night as Willenhall hosted their biggest crowd of the season. They had done a job on us in one of the many cup competitions and were up for doing it again. That was obvious from the start, but we were five games undefeated and had practically our strongest side out. Their game was clear from kick off. Strong, big and physical they played a tough style and dictated from the beginning. We played well when allowed to but that wasn't often.

Bernard wants to play flowing passing football, and at times we did just that prior to being scythed down by a back four who had a plan and did it well. My mistake was sitting between Lee Carter and Dave Topping. After 15 minutes I was deaf from the noise they made. We were sitting behind a brick wall which was probably strong, considering the number of times that Lee punched it. He kicked every ball, made every cross and lived every moment. Then it happened like it always does Stuart ran from his line and slipped, Leon and Duane were still on the bus, well they would have been if we'd travelled on one, and Willenhall scored.

This shouldn't be a problem as we're good at being 1-0 down, in fact it doesn't seem natural when we're not. We played, we ran and we ran some more straight into a back four that made Tony Adams look like a wimp. Long balls, hit and hope became the game every time they headed them out.

Then came the second half. We carried on where we left off, playing great football across the park, but rarely in their box. Hope came from a couple of free kicks, but an honest man would say we never looked like scoring. Alfie came on and ran like a man with a point to prove but caused little trouble. So that's the way it stayed: 1-0. I didn't try to talk to Bernard afterwards - what was there to say?

# 7. January

## 3 January: Home to Kendal Town

Kendal beat us 4-2 when we went to the land of mint cake, so with this in mind, a woeful performance at Willenhall and the thought of going back to work tomorrow I wasn't exactly looking forward to today. The biting north wind and the sunless sky didn't help either.

The old-timers in the Scrap Yard End were starting to lose patience as they mumbled home truths about the team having no edge and stories about the time when boots were high and legs got broken. I don't claim to know whether they are right or wrong, but I do know that some consistency is needed.

Kick off: we made a good start with energy and pace, we ran at them again and again, but then they broke down the right. Deano chased, he caught his man and cleared. Our fans all clapped. We came back with a cross into the box, a scrambled Kyle shot, it went wide, and the crowd got noisy. Into the box again, Luke shot but couldn't make a good contact. Their goalkeeper turned it wide. A corner, they cleared and the crowd was loud. I didn't want to say it out loud but we were playing well, Bernard looked concerned, but then he always does.

Twenty minutes in, Sean made a captain's cross into the box, Kyle bent to head it, for a moment 1,400 people held their breath, had it touched him? Yes it had! 1-0. "Come on you whites!" I felt I could touch the noise.

Next Leon hit a free kick as sweet as any I will ever see: 2-0. We were on a roll. Leon is a good player and a big character. There have been times when I thought he seemed to forget he was part of a team, and times when I thought he needed a kick up the ass but as the ball hit the net I was glad he was there.

The Scrap Yard End was silent. I think they were in shock "2-0, this isn't right, we come here to have a good moan," I heard one old-timer say. Alfie had been on from the start, but hadn't scored for a very long time. Some say it was luck that he just ran onto a rebound. Who cares? It was 3-0 and still Bernard wouldn't sit down.

Five minutes later normal service was returned. The ball bounced high. Leon thought Stuart had got it and Stuart, yes that's right, thought Leon had got it: 3-1.

Now there are times when I think that Alfie is more ornament than use and there are times when I think he's in the same game as everybody else, just five seconds behind it, but there is one thing no one can doubt: he's fast. When he runs like he can, anything can happen. Today he won us a penalty, 4-1, he went off to a standing ovation.

Oh well, let's see what next Saturday brings.

Telford midfielder Luke McNally in the thick of the action against Kendal Town at the Bucks Head.

Missed! Kyle Perry, Neil Howarth and Damien Charie can't watch as Perry's header goes narrowly wide of the Eastwood Town goal. Telford won 2-0.

Unibond Northern League Division One 6 January 2005
(Top 10)

| | | P | Pts |
|---|---|---|---|
| 1. | North Ferriby | 23 | 46 |
| 2. | Ilkeston Town | 22 | 45 |
| 3. | Willenhall Town | 22 | 42 |
| 4. | Gresley Rovers | 21 | 41 |
| **5.** | **AFC Telford U** | **24** | **38** |
| 6. | Eastwood Town | 22 | 35 |
| 7. | Stocksbridge PS | 23 | 35 |
| 8. | Ossett Albion | 22 | 34 |
| 9. | Kendal Town | 21 | 34 |
| 10. | Brigg Town | 22 | 32 |

## 8 January: Home to Eastwood Town

All I remember from when we played Eastwood Town was the rain, the sloping pitch, the cold and losing. Which is probably enough to remember about any match, and now they were coming to us unbeaten in eight games.

Gale force winds and floods had cut off the north of the country and most of Carlisle was underwater, but here it was just very cold. Even with last week's win, Bernard was still getting some criticism in the local paper, so the wind probably seemed a little more intense to him than the rest of us. Neil Howarth was back after his suspension, but Alfie was out injured. Nick Smith was in the squad, but was probably on his way back to his own club unless he got a hat-trick today, which is unlikely from his starting position: the bench.

Still, Bernard was sticking to his plan, passing football, no long balls; you had to admire his courage, but 10 minutes in we were running around in circles. Then after 30 minutes Luke shot hard from just outside the box. For a moment it was going wide, but Kyle came from nowhere: 1-0. His 16th goal in 20 matches; to quote Ron Atkinson "He's so cool his boots are on fire."

One day Bernard will realise that the box painted around the dugout is where he is supposed to stand, not a start line to run from every time we score. In fact he's normally better positioned that the linesman by the time he's stopped.

For the rest of the half we battered them, I just think that they were not used to playing on a level pitch. The second goal was going to come and it did, but not until we almost managed to let them get even. Neil put his foot on the ball and slipped, but Brockie thought that Neil had it. In fact Eastwood did. Well they did until they shot at the empty goal. Typical, we thought, another stupid goal given away, but then Jack Cudworth came from nowhere and cleared. I'll never comment about his waistline again. It really does seem that we've got luck on our side now.

Little Deano has always been everyone's favourite and today he was on a roll, charging down their left like a ferret on heat. At the third attempt he found a gap and Damien made it 2-0.

Close to the end, Luke had another go, not quite this time but his first goal can't be far away. Just to seal their fate Eastwood managed to get two players sent off.

Full time: we had won. Days like this don't get any better.

## 15 January: Away to Kidsgrove Athletic

We left the ground at midday and as usual stopped to pick up most of the team on the way. Alfie was in the right place at the right time, I wondered if it was an omen. Shakey drank three bottles of some flavoured milk drink before we got off the M54, then ate a packet of Jaffa Cakes to soak it up. Lee sat at the front, because he's the chairman, and looked at his copy of *The Times*. Al the driver nearly got up to 50mph at one time, but slowed down because of his heart. Bernard looked relaxed and seemed more interested in the cricket score.

I looked down the aisle of the bus, everyone now has their seat, but today the lads were quiet, Stuart and Sean sat at the table but weren't even bothering with the never-ending game of cards. Alfie was up to mischief on the back seat and Duane was having none of it; Leon was out injured so he had no one to play with. Kyle sat alone and stared out of the window, Deano looked happy, but then he always does. Luke relaxed as he nodded off to sleep; the rest plugged their ears with Discmans and nodded to sounds of their own. I know that when the season is over this journey is one I will miss.

We lost 4-2 last time we came here. It was a wet cold night; the ground was in the middle of a housing estate and the car park the size of a postage stamp. Guess what? The ground hasn't moved, the car park seemed even smaller and the weather was bloody awful. Last October, just like now, we were on a roll except then it was a losing roll. Stuart has saved us many times, so it's unfair of me to remember more than anything from that night we came here, his poor clearance that rolled to the feet of a Kidsgrove player who looked embarrassed as he tapped it into an open goal. But as they say, the ref and the goalkeepers are the only ones not allowed to make mistakes.

From the off they seemed to be having slightly the better of us, but we came back and scored. The man so good they named him thrice, David Andrewartha made a great pass to Damien who scored off the post. They equalised just after half-time. Damien went off and Alfie came on and scored, (look Alfie I remembered to mentioned it). I thought revenge would be ours, but they scored with two minutes to go. Hard to bear, we should have won. If ever anyone deserved a goal it was Luke. He's come so close now in so many matches, but close doesn't count.

Half of this team is different to the one who played that cold night last October, the mentality of all of this team is different. We are in the play-off places, fourth in the league, but teams around us have games in hand. This team as it is now would easily win promotion; it wouldn't need to have played more games to be where it is. But this isn't the team who started the season. We turned the corner the day we lost at Ilkeston, but did we turn it early enough?

## 22 January: Home to Stocksbridge Park Steels

So far this season we had managed to get ourselves knocked out of every cup competition at the first attempt so getting a bye into the quarter-finals of the Unibond League Chairman's Cup was probably the only way we were going to get there. The question now was: could we make the semi-final?

It was a cold afternoon, the grey sky threatened snow and a northerly wind cut through many layers of clothing with ease. Bernard looked relaxed, he had a good choice to make, a good choice for him that is. "Do I play Leon or Glenn or Dave?" He thought out loud. I didn't think he was actually too worried about my opinion, so I didn't answer. It's a good problem to have when you think of the starting line up he had to choose from less than 12 weeks before.

I think Brin had put Red Bull in the pre-match drinks the way we went at Stocksbridge for the first 20 minutes. It seemed obvious that we would score, but it wouldn't have been the first time we didn't score when we should have. And then we did score and very hard work we made of it too. It started with a free kick from Jack Cudworth which they cleared, and we put it back in again and they cleared it again, so we put it back in again and they cleared it again. Dave Andrewartha put it back in again and Damien headed down over the 'keeper but short of the line; the ball seemed to go into slow motion as it bounced up and gently kissed the back of the net.

Round two: they came out like men possessed and forced Stuart into a run of good saves before they scored. Then it was pretty well even for the rest of the half. As full-time approached, we had a flurry of shots but it just wasn't to be. By now the sky was gin clear and the temperature well below zero. People started to leave; no one had told them there would be extra time and penalties and how could they know: our new club had never got this far in a cup competition.

Full-time came, the teams changed ends and off we all went again. We ran and they ran - this was good football. Extra time was running out as they announced that penalties would be at the Naggington end. If the ground had been a boat it would have capsized as a tide of people flowed down the stadium. This was an amazing piece of fate that put them all in

Dancing Damien! Damien Charie celebrates his goal at Kidsgrove Athletic.

exactly the right position to watch Luke McNally pick up the ball on the right and run at Stockbridge like a whippet on heat; as he beat the first defender we all took notice, as he beat the second, 1,000 people stood up, as he beat the third 1,000 people stopped breathing as he beat the 'keeper 1,000 people screamed.

Bernard almost had a Barry Fry moment and had to be held back by the fourth official. But a goal by his son in the dying minutes of extra time, not just a goal, but a great goal. What a feeling. No one could imagine the pride he must have been feeling, no writer could write that kind of drama, and just for a moment it didn't seem quite so cold.

## 29 January: Away to Belper Town

Things got off to a good start - no one got lost on the way to the bus and we made it to the ground with no unintended detours. We had a new driver this week so managed to break the 30mph mark on occasions. When we got to Belper we did stop at a bus stop. Where else, but a bus stop I suppose, to ask directions, but we managed this without circling the town five times.

Belper is a pretty town in the Peak District, quiet and slow. It had its claims to fame and at one time had been a world centre of nail making. Why nails should come from this place, I have no idea, but they are proud enough of this to call their football team the Nailers.

Today was the kind of match we should win. Belper were in the bottom five, we were in the top five. We'd only lost one game in our last five; Belper had only won one in their last five. Bernard looked pensive and it was no wonder. We had to win matches like this as a matter of course if promotion was to be a realistic prospect. The team was pretty well full strength and had all played together more than once. I looked at Bernard across the pitch; he gives little away, but today he just looked a little concerned.

To start with all looked well; we were on top and were battering them. But then we should have been. We were the better side, the in-form side. After about 30 minutes we won a free kick on the edge of their area. Kyle was up for taking it, somehow he managed to have an argument with the ref when it was our kick and he was taking it, but that's Kyle. Then he hit it without a run up. He looked angry, his kick seemed more petulant than aimed, but who cares? 1-0.

Stuart is a good 'keeper and I like him, it's impossible not to like him. He's a genuine person, but there are times when I wish he would shout a bit more. With minutes to go to half-time, Belper had a corner. Stuart caught it easily, but was pushed over the line: 1-1. No one thought it was a goal, not even their directors, unfortunately the ref did. Stuart just shrugged; I know an argument would have done no good, but then...?

For the next 45 minutes they just punted long balls across the ground with no real plan or purpose to them, just long kicks. And guess what we did? We played long balls across the ground with no real plan or purpose. They dragged us down and we let them. You could see the frustration in Bernard's face, we could play better than this and he knew it.

The afternoon grew dark and the lights came on as the final whistle blew, the lads looked like a team that had been beaten. They walked like a beaten team; beaten by not playing the way they can play.

It is not that far to Belper, but the journey home seemed a long way. The silence on the bus spoke like a scream. Being beaten by a better team is bearable, being beaten by a lucky goal is unfortunate, but being beaten by yourself is unacceptable. Oh well, here's to next week.

Telford defender Duane Courtney battles for the ball with a Belper Town player.

# 8. February

## 5 February: Home to Ilkeston Town

It was 'fill the stadium day'. Dave Topping, the operations director did not look happy. In fact he hadn't looked happy since the idea was suggested. I don't understand; what's the problem with bussing in 1,900 children? We broke the Unibond League gate record easily; also we could probably be in the *Guinness Book of Records* for the biggest crèche in the world.

Was it a bit contrived to give tickets away and bus in the kids? Probably it was, but who cares it made for a great atmosphere. Lez aka Benny the Buck was having the time of his life; after all there was an audience of 1,900 for him. Imagine describing your weekend to a stranger, "Well I dressed up as a seven foot deer and rolled about on the ground in front of 2,000 kids..."

We had beaten Ilkeston away, could we do it at home? They were second in the table, with games in hand, for a reason. The atmosphere was building before the match had started and it probably had more to do with Nigel Jemson warming up in his old Shrewsbury Town top than the kids in the stand.

We went at them for the first 10 minutes, then they went at us and then it settled down into a not particularly good game of football. Even Kyle was managing to stay on his feet. It got quite interesting on the press bench as Stuart sliced at a clearance and managed to hit three journalists in one go. And none of them had written anything nasty about him - yet. Deano looked alive with some good runs and an in-swinging cross that almost scored on its own. But mostly a lot of grit and running seemed to be coming to nothing.

The kids kept on singing, the regulars kept on moaning and Bernard kept on shouting. I wonder when he will realise that they can't hear him. But at half-time it was 0-0. The second half started like the first had ended: 22 heroes kept on running, courage, grit and determination was scattered over the pitch like bodies on a battlefield, but no one could score. They had the best of the chances, but a diving save from Stuart saved the day after Neil managed to turn an Ilkeston corner straight towards our own net.

An hour into the match and the children was becoming quiet. For most it was the first football match they had been to, you could almost see a young face look up and say, "But daddy when will someone score a goal thing?". Ilkeston were having the better of it when Stuart cleared the length of the pitch the ball bounced once and Ilkeston's keeper caught it. He had a point to prove and cleared back up the pitch to Stuart who, guess what? Cleared back down the pitch again except this time it landed short of the box and bounced straight over their defender who had come to collect it. Kyle ran goal-side of him and managed to stay on his feet long enough to side-foot it in to the net; all planned at the last training session of course.

The score board flashed "Birmingham City 0 Manchester United 2" a slight jeer rose from the crowd. "Manchester City 0 Chelsea 0" a few clapped, most nodded in approval. Then flashed and a whole sentence appeared: "You're not going to like this!"

They even had the apostrophe in the right place, a slight confusion descended on the crowd: "Shrewsbury Town 4 Leyton Orient 1". The silence was tangible.

Ilkeston tried to come back, but never quite got back into the game. 1-0 we won, the kids sung and most were happy. In many ways it had been a traditional non-League game: hard and gritty. The football hadn't been attractive, flowing, skilful or inspired, but it had been professional and tough.

Unibond Northern League Division One 7 February 2005
(Top 10)

| | | P | Pts |
|---|---|---|---|
| 1. | North Ferriby | 27 | 56 |
| 2. | Ilkeston Town | 25 | 51 |
| 3. | Willenhall Town | 25 | 49 |
| **4.** | **AFC Telford U** | **28** | **46** |
| 5. | Gresley Rovers | 25 | 43 |
| 6. | Brigg Town | 26 | 42 |
| 7. | Kendal Town | 24 | 41 |
| 8. | Mossley | 26 | 41 |
| 9. | Eastwood Town | 26 | 39 |
| 10. | Stocksbridge PS | 26 | 36 |

## 12 February: Away to Stocksbridge Park Steels

People from Sheffield think that Stocksbridge is near Manchester and people from Manchester think it's near Sheffield. In fact it is on the side of the Little Don Valley on the edge of the Peak District. The view over the Peaks would have been stunning if it hadn't been for the low cloud, gale-force winds and driving rain.

We arrived in Stocksbridge and a board nailed to a tree advertised the match, but no one could see anything that looked like a football club. We didn't know then that the football ground was at the top of a mountain. Slowly we began to climb, and given the speed Al normally drives, you should understand that we were now being overtaken by old men on bikes going uphill. Then we stopped; a hairpin-bend had to be negotiated. Slowly Al began to manoeuvre around the turn. The final scene from *The Italian Job* sprang to mind as the coach stalled. I had a mental picture of Bernard crawling down the bus trying to rescue a pallet load of gold. Once around the bend we crawled up the hill occasionally touching 10mph. The bus began to labour as the oxygen in the air became thinner.

Telford goalkeeper Stuart Brock signs autographs.

'Fill the stadium day': Telford versus Ilkeston Town.

The Stocksbridge keeper wins the ball ahead of United's Duane Courtney.

Shakey announced that we were playing at the "Stadium of height." It was a funny line, so he repeated it another 50-or-so times just to make sure that he got the maximum number of laughs from his joke.

I wouldn't say that the visibility was bad, but all we could see of the ground was the floodlights rising out of a sea of mist. As it cleared I thought the pitch was an open-air swimming bath, there was so much water; but at least that meant we couldn't see the four inches of mud that was supposed to be the playing surface. Obviously no one but the brave or the foolish would attempt to play football on a pitch like that.

Their manager wanted to call it off, the ref wasn't too certain, Bernard had no doubt. "Bloody great, let's get out there." It was obvious, what had happened to him, nine months in charge of AFC Telford had sent him completely around a bend sharper than the one at the bottom of the hill.

The wind was probably touching 30mph as we kicked off and we were playing with it to our backs. Their 'keeper couldn't even get the ball out of his own half. All his clearances seemed to hit an invisible wall and then bounce back at him. Almost all of the play happened in one small corner of the pitch. The weather simply stopped anyone moving out of this space and when they did Stocksbridge scored, 1-0.

Five minutes later Luke made a wind assisted run down the right, and crossed into the box just as Alfie arrived. The thing about Alfie is he just so totally infuriates you: for complete matches you get the feeling he's more of a decorative figure than a useful player, then suddenly he does something so skilful and cool he makes Rooney look like an amateur, 1-1.

Stuart looked cold and alone in front of his goal for most of the half. Bernard stood in front of his box soaked to the skin shouting into the wind and the rest of us just got cold. By the second half the rain had stopped and a rainbow arched across the valley. The wind was almost gale-force and now Stuart was kicking into it, and when high balls didn't get the ball past the half way line he tried low ones and when that didn't work he gave up and passed it to Neil. By now very little of what was happening had anything to do with football. After 60 minutes it looked more like a mud fight; all that was needed was two women in bikinis.

With about 25 minutes to go we won a corner, Deano chipped it across the goalmouth and Kyle hit it goalwards, but that man Alfie popped up again to give it a helping boot and make it two for the day. Kyle was talking to him by the time the match was over, but at that moment if looks could kill, Alfie would have been on the way to the undertaker's. It was 2-1 to Telford.

We had won. All we had to do now was abseil from the ground back down the mountain, get the bus back around the hairpin and drive home as the radio was repeating advice that only essential journeys should be made. It took the first 40 minutes of the bus ride to get feeling back in our feet. This is a day I will tell my grandchildren about and mightily bored they will be.

Unibond Northern League Division One 16 February 2005
(Top 10)

|     |                | P   | Pts |
| --- | -------------- | --- | --- |
| 1.  | North Ferriby  | 29  | 62  |
| 2.  | Ilkeston Town  | 25  | 51  |
| 3.  | Willenhall Town | 25 | 49  |
| **4.** | **AFC Telford U** | **29** | **49** |
| 5.  | Brigg Town     | 27  | 45  |
| 6.  | Gresley Rovers | 26  | 43  |
| 7.  | Mossley        | 26  | 41  |
| 8.  | Kendal Town    | 25  | 41  |
| 9.  | Eastwood Town  | 27  | 39  |
| 10. | Woodley Sports | 24  | 36  |

## 19 February: Home to Woodley Sports

Standing at the Bucks Head on a bitter cold February day as flurries of snow race past the floodlights driven by a northerly wind, the end of the season seemed too far away to be a concern, but there are just 13 league games left in the campaign. Bernard keeps telling me we have points on the board, which is true, but we still have to win all our matches and have Ilkeston or Brigg Town do us a favour with timely losses.

Every game is a 'massive game' for us from now on. One loss and we are out of it and that's without the play-offs or cup games. Today in the cold as wet snow filtered through grey cloud, and our end of season begins, some fellow called Wayne is playing at Everton and there's been a lot of fuss about that but I can't think why. It's nowhere as near an important match as AFC Telford United versus Woodley Sports.

Somewhere else Brentford from League One are playing Southampton in the FA Cup, not bad but 20 years ago this weekend it was also United playing Everton; Telford United that is. And they were a lot further behind Everton than Brentford are Southampton. Many of the men who played then are here today. Fathers and grandfathers, they sit in the posh seats and balance small children on their knees. Their hair might be a little greyer and their joints a bit stiffer than they were that weekend two decades ago, but the memory of what they did is still written large in the history of football in Telford.

Men who know nothing of the game can pull down the stands and bankrupt a business, but there is more to a football club than a signature on a cheque or figures on a balance sheet. So maybe as the other United speed along the M62 they should glance south down the M6 as they pass, notice the Bucks Head in the distance and tell Malcolm Glazer where to put his dollars.

After last week at Stocksbridge the New Bucks Head felt like the New Wembley Stadium. Unfortunately the football was no warmer, it just wasn't a great game, we weren't playing badly and neither were they. It

Kyle Perry in action against Woodley Sports at the Bucks Head.

just wasn't gripping stuff. Dave Andrewartha and Jack Cudworth were having good games and Duane Courtney was as solid as ever, but mostly not much was happening. Leon was back on the bench for the first time in weeks, but sat in the cold watching Dave play a good game probably didn't make him feel any warmer. He was sat in the same seat that Carl Tranter had occupied for the last couple of months and he's now on loan to Bromsgrove Rovers. The whole afternoon was a bit sad really, given the heroes sat watching the game.

The second half picked up at bit, to say the least Bernard generally isn't one for the Alex Ferguson hairdryer treatment or kicking football boots, but I got the feeling that today the air was a pale shade of blue. Two minutes into the half Deano crossed into the box, but David miss-hit it, the ball bounced around like a homeless pinball when Kyle arrived like an express train with no brakes, taking the ball, the 'keeper, several lumps of turf and himself over the line. 1,500 people stood up. So did the linesman: offside. It was impossible to tell if he was correct, but the man in black was adamant. For the next 15 minutes we battered them. We were shooting for fun, even Sean got in on the act with a lob over the keeper. It was probably harder to hit the bar than the net but never mind. Five minutes later and David crossed to Kyle who headed over the 'keeper. This time he was onside: 1-0.

Stuart rushed off his line for a clearance, as he does once in every match, but the ball went straight to one of their players who was most certainly in an offside position. He was so put off by the linesman not flagging that he hit the post and missed the rebound.

Sean got clattered and his toe was broken. They were down to 10 men, Luke limped off, Leon came on and promptly got himself booked. We hung on, we won; we have no other options we had to win all the teams around us won. There are 12 matches to go.

## 26 February: Away to Clitheroe

It was a cold day as we gathered at the Bucks Head. There weren't that many of us, most get on just before we join the M6 and Alfie gets on when he can find the pick-up point. Shakey and Lee were going up in cars so that left almost no one at ground. "Are we picking Kyle up at the pub or in Featherstone?" Derek asked. No one seemed to know; after all he is only the leading goalscorer, I suppose we could manage without him.

Sean was travelling, but was out with a broken toe and Luke had pulled his hamstring so stayed in bed. But at least they weren't the kind of problems that we had in November when Bernard used to be embarrassed at the choice of players he had to put on the bench then.

All aboard, we headed north; Clitheroe isn't quite in the Lake District, and is a long way from Manchester. Blackburn is the biggest place local to it, so really it's one of those places that isn't really anywhere.

The usual gang were playing their never-ending game of cards; Alfie and Leon were up to no good on the back seat. The rest just slept or stare out of the window. Bernard tried to sit down and read a newspaper, there is an article about Mourinho and tomorrow's Carling Cup Final. He starts it three times and never gets past the first paragraph; he's always too full of nervous energy on a match day. It usually takes him the first hour to relax. We chat about what he wants from the rest of the season, we had 12 matches including today. "Twelve wins." he smiled. I asked what he would take if he was given it now. He settled on seven wins and four or five draws. Given our recent form that didn't sound unreasonable.

The driver said that we've made good time so we stop at a service station. It's like a school outing: Derek, Brin and Bernard head for a table and a cup of tea. The team go straight for the pool table and the machines with the bright flashing lights. You can hear them from 100 yards way, but it's all good natured. Neil and Sean try to maintain a distance as the coach and captain, but still get pulled into the laughter.

Back on the bus we had to have three head counts until we're certain everyone's here. We stopped in Clitheroe's main street and could see the floodlights, but not the ground. Bernard phoned for directions. "Right we've got to walk from here, down the street and turn right by the salmon coloured house." He shouts down the bus.

"Salmon?" a voice from the back calls, "Is that like orange?"

With each of us carrying a bit of kit, we trooped down the street and file across the road past a light orange house and stop in the backyard of a wine merchants. Then Brin notices an alleyway behind the orange house. Clitheroe's ground is surrounded on all four sides by houses; they have ladders ready to climb over the fences to get the balls back. The playing surface looks like a potato field. The stands resemble a shed. The director's box is a shed. The whole place is wonderful; it is the personification of non-league football.

We were on a roll: three straight wins and seven games without defeat. They were close to the bottom of the league without a win in five games. This kind of match that requires a professional non-complacent approach otherwise it will jump up and bite you hard.

The sky cleared and the sun came through, a large snow capped hill, similar to our Wrekin, overlooked the town. We kicked off a few minutes early and less than 10 minutes later Alfie flicked the ball into their box, but Kyle put it inches wide, we were all over them like a bad rash. The game was going to be ours, everyone relaxed and slowly our rash retreated. On 15 minutes, Kyle was pulled down by their keeper; well it looked that way, and won us a penalty. He stood and looked at the ball, but his body language looked wrong, I knew he wouldn't score. He hit it low: their keeper dived and parried, he hit the rebound hard and wide. There was no reaction from Bernard. He knew - it was too easy to save. We just didn't look convincing, and that's the way it stayed.

On 40 minutes Clitheroe crossed high into our box. Stuart punched but fell over, the ball fell to them: 1-0. The next five minutes happened in a blur, as the whistle went the look on Bernard's face said it all, the way he walked spoke volumes. Lee had only smiled once during the half when the Clitheroe support asked: "Can we play you every week?"

Whatever was said worked, but not enough. We had the ball and passed it a lot, but never really looked like scoring, I lost count of the number of corners we won, we were battering them, but they just stood and took it. They dug in to defend their lead; every corner went into their box and came out again. Just after the hour Leon hit a free kick hard and low into their area. It came out again, but this time it rolled to Jack who hit it and hoped: 1-1. The cheer was muted. We all knew at heart we probably didn't deserve it.

It was a long way home that night; the game of cards continued but was quiet. The cool gang at the back were not so loud. Bernard never did get around to reading the article on Mourinho. I don't think that he expected one of the "four or five draws..." to be used up to day.

Damien Charie and Alfie Carter celebrate with Jack Cudworth after his equaliser against Clitheroe.

# 9. March

|     |                | P  | Pts |
| --- | -------------- | -- | --- |
| 1.  | North Ferriby  | 31 | 66  |
| 2.  | Willenhall Town | 29 | 61 |
| 3.  | Ilkeston Town  | 27 | 57  |
| **4.** | **AFC Telford U** | **31** | **53** |
| 5.  | Kendal Town    | 29 | 50  |
| 6.  | Brigg Town     | 28 | 48  |
| 7.  | Gresley Rovers | 28 | 47  |
| 8.  | Mossley        | 28 | 42  |
| 9.  | Eastwood Town  | 28 | 42  |
| 10. | Woodley Sports | 26 | 39  |

### 5 March: Home to Kidsgrove Athletic

After we got knocked out of the FA Cup, the FA Trophy and the Unibond League Cup there was only one consolation cup left - the Chairman's Cup.

We were at home to Kidsgrove. That had got to be a good omen - after all you can't play a team four times in one season without beating them once. Can you?

Lost 3-1. Who the hell wants to win the Chairman's Cup anyway?

### 12 March: Home to Chorley

The sky was very blue and high white clouds scudded past, driven by a cold wind. Bernard smiled as he stood in the tunnel and looked out over the pitch. He was very aware of the hopes that are pinned on him. With an hour to kick off and already over 500 of the faithful are scattered around the ground. Some of the team are out on the pitch warming up. There was no mistaking that it is match day. We walked out into the centre and start dropping cones to make a rectangle. It is only when you have stood in the middle of the Buck's Head and Stocksbridge and Rocester that you can make a comparison of the grounds. Bernard keeps saying that teams raise their game when they come here and there have been a few times when I've thought "Yeah, yeah, we've heard that one all ready." But the other grounds in the League make this look like the Millennium Stadium and today watching it fill from the centre I could see what Bernard meant.

The rectangle laid out. We stand and look around, Bernard asked about the Arsenal versus Bolton Wanderers match, but didn't hear the answer. He's like this every match day; trying to behave normally, but his mind always flitting back to game. He's not a rude man, but suddenly he wandered off mid-sentence, forgetting everything except the next 90 minutes. I walked away unnoticed.

It was two minutes to three, the shadow of the main stand drew a straight line down the pitch, all of the players were in position; the referee raised the whistle to his lips. But something was not right; the goalkeepers were at the wrong ends. Stuart laughed to himself and like his counterpart began a long run to the other end; they swapped a sporting thumb's up as they passed.

From the off they ran at us. It was not looking good; within two minutes they had split our back four and shot wide. Then Duane saved the day with some excellent defending. The Scrap Yard End wasn't silent, but wasn't not that vocal either. Then, against the run of play, Stuart cleared a long ball. It bounced to the left of their box and was chipped in; we had a new boy Darren Alexander up front. The chip landed at his feet but he was being closed down by two Chorley players. He carried on running through a narrowing gap. I think he hit it or was it a clearance that went the wrong way, who knows? But their 'keeper stood helpless as the ball slowly arched over his finger tips and into the net. Own goal? Who cares? 1-0.

Now I think that Leon can have a bit of an attitude, and there are times when I can see why Bernard has leaves him out of the team, but today I could see nothing but a hero. We shot and it was saved, but the clearance was short. Played back in it bounced and fell to Leon with the centre of their box was packed with blue shirts. Anyone else would have passed, but not Leon. With total confidence he scooped it up and over, over the blue shirts, over the goalkeeper and into the net. Was he selfish? Who cares: 2-0.

Now we were singing "Who are you? Who are you?" Then we fell silent, but no they hadn't scored, for the next 10 minutes was an exhibition of footballing skill, we passed, we anticipated, we were skilful, it was total football: long balls, short balls. I was mesmerised. Another five minutes and I thought Chorley looked like a pub team, hacking at everything. Luke was brought down in the box: a clear penalty I thought. The ref waved play on. They were lashing out at nothing; it was getting very physical; the yellow card came out. A free kick on the edge of their box, Leon stepped up to take it; slowly the ball cut an arc high over the wall. Was the free kick given to make amends for the penalty we weren't given? Who knows? 3-0. All this and there were still 10 minutes to half-time.

Part two began and gradually it became a kicking competition: each other, not the ball that is. Neil had been having a quiet game up to this point, effective but quiet. When he ran back to a loose ball, their man slid in, missed the ball and hit his ankle. Neil stood looking down, they both began shouting. I can't lip read, but I don't think they were enquiring about each other's health. Then they were face-to-face, nose-to-nose. I remembered the last time this happened he got himself a three match ban. He seemed to have learnt his lesson as their player put both hands on his chest. His only move was to fall backwards. They were down to 10 men. Did he deserve to get sent off? Who cares? 11 versus 10.

We were 3-0 up and they were down to 10 men. The next 45 minutes should have been a cruise, but there are times when watching Telford you can never be certain which team you are going to watch. One week they are committed, a tough battling team, the next a skilful side playing a fast passing game and the next; well it's probably best not to describe the team that they are sometimes. Though this week was the first time I think all three teams have played in the same match. After a poor start we battled and scored, we were committed. After the second goal we could have been Arsenal, for a moment the beauty of their game left a lot silent, and then it was now. Now the lads that had run out were wearing the same shirts so I guess it was the same team, they just played differently. The polite description is to say we lost our shape. "This is rubbish" to quote the man three rows in front of me. A better team would have hurt us. We hung on, we used all three subs, did the score flattered us? Does it matter? We won.

## 15 March: Away to Woodley Sports

Woodley, being just south of Manchester made this one of the shorter journeys of the season. It had rained a bit at home but nothing like it must have in Woodley. The only time I've ever seen a pitch like this one is on 1970s footage of matches re-run for yet another documentary on George Best or for an obituary of an old time player who never earned in his life what Rio Ferdinand did yesterday. To say it was nothing more than black mud would be an exaggeration.

Winning is getting to be a habit; talk of automatic promotion has now replaced talk of the play-offs, which in turn replaced talk of sacking Bernard. As always we had to win tonight, but just under a month ago we'd made hard work of it when Woodley came to the Bucks Head. On the long bus journey to Stocksbridge, Bernard told me we were due to give someone a battering and today would be it. We came away from there with a 2-1 win after a battle in the mud. He had said the same on the even longer ride to Clitheroe. We were lucky to get a draw there. I don't recall him saying it on the way tonight; perhaps he thought it would never happen?

35th minute: David Andrewartha crossed into the box with the accuracy of David Beckham while running at full speed and under pressure from what seemed like 20 Woodley players all carrying machine guns and knives. Meanwhile Roy Jordan has found the gift of making himself invisible – reappearing at the far post just as the crossed ball

83

arrived to head it home: 1-0. This was without doubt a worthy contender for goal of the century.

At the start of the second half, Woodley were still thinking about their half-time cup of Bovril when Alfie Carter arrived in their box. It was so open that it was as if he had been sent a gold embossed invitation by royal messenger. He got there just as another cross from a footballing genius, who I think will be England captain one day, David Andrewartha, arrived for him to make the score 2-0.

With two minutes left, the captain who makes Roy Keane look like an unambitious dilettante who cares little for success, Sean Parrish, placed a perfectly weighted free-kick. It was so perfect that Jonny Wilkinson would have gasped with envy at his skill. Right into the box and onto the chest of that man again - Alfie Carter - who even though facing the wrong way turned and strolled through their defence as if he were escorting a lady through the park, to slot home: 3-0.

In the last minute, Alfie, by now struggling with a groin injury so painful he should be given a medal for bravery, side-stepped their defenders in the same style as Ryan Giggs. Then he scored his third of the night: 4-0.

And apologies to Sean and Glenn that I couldn't find the name of a Welsh rugby player as good as Jonny Wilkinson.

## 19 March: Away to Mossley

It was a warm fine morning, and things could not be better, we'd stuffed Woodley 4-0 and we hadn't lost - in the league - this year. Okay, half of the first choice team were injured, but that was a minor worry. Dave Topping looked at Lee and asked "Have we been third in the league before this season?" Lee laughed: "I can't remember Telford ever being third in any league ever."

"There's an accident on the M6 so I'm going up the A49," the bus driver said; this wasn't a big issue, it's just that we pick up most of the team on the way to the M6. We might have been on a winning run but this would have meant Shakey being in goal and Lee up front.

So we moved the pick up point to Cosford, this should have been no problem, but these are footballers. Twenty phone calls later we were at Cosford waiting and waiting. Some were now driving up, mobile phones were turned off and other didn't know where Cosford was, but at least the sun was shining and we did get a great tour of the Cheshire countryside after we did eventually leave.

At 1.30pm we were still an hour away from the ground. At 2.15pm Shakey phoned the team sheet through. The referee would not put the kick off back. Bernard was still smiling, but his teeth were gritted. By 2.20pm things looked better; at least we were in Mossley. All we had to do now was find the ground. At 2.25pm the driver was asking directions and at 2.26pm he was turning a 52 seat bus around in Mossley High Street.

Duane's always come across as a bright lad and is usually quite quiet. Today he showed how bright he is. As we arrived in Mossley he suddenly changed into a clown, leaping around the bus, throwing water in players' faces and making a complete fool of himself. Now given the size of Stuart Brock you've got to be pretty confident - or mad - to throw water in his face. The bus was hot and everyone was sleepy until Duane began his act. Five minutes later they were all up for it.

For a moment I thought he might have gone a bit far when he shouted that arriving late was better than having a speech from the gaffer. Bernard tried very hard not to laugh, but it was funny. An old man limped past the bus wrapped in a coat, hat, scarf and muffler. "Look it's Glenn Tolley." Sean called, by now the atmosphere was more like a comedy club than a football bus.

We arrived at 2.35. They say that the ground is one of the highest in the country and the view was incredible, but another problem seemed to be looming as the tunnel was the narrowest I have ever seen. How was Jack going to get onto the pitch?

We were up for it, we ran like men obsessed, but it was Mossley who shot wide first, but on seven minutes a poor back header from a Mossley defender dropped short as Darren Alexander ran in and hit it: 1-0. A muted cheer stuttered from the followers. The supporters' bus hadn't arrived yet. A long way to travel to miss the first goal.

At the half hour they split us up the centre with pace. It had to be a goal, but Stuart came off his line and the shot went just high and wide. Maybe we had used up all our bad luck for the day on the journey there.

Mossley is the only team we've played this year with a current international in its line-up, okay he plays for Guyana, not one of the world's great footballing nations, but he's still an international.

Many years ago now Manchester United came to the Bucks Head and Ryan Giggs took the mickey. Today, his younger brother, Rhodri, was on the park and hit a beautiful volley on the turn that his brother would have been proud of.

We didn't play well, in fact we were awful at times, but we hung on. "A good team is one that can go away, play badly and win 1-0," Bernard said to me later. I asked him about automatic promotion; he wouldn't comment, but his mouth turned up to a slight smile. Perhaps it really is possible?

Unibond Northern League Division One 22 March 2005
(Top 10)

|     |                 | P  | Pts |
| --- | --------------- | -- | --- |
| 1.  | North Ferriby   | 34 | 67  |
| 2.  | Willenhall Town | 32 | 64  |
| **3.** | **AFC Telford U** | **34** | **62** |
| 4.  | Ilkeston Town   | 32 | 62  |
| 5.  | Kendal Town     | 33 | 57  |
| 6.  | Gresley Rovers  | 32 | 53  |
| 7.  | Eastwood Town   | 33 | 51  |
| 8.  | Brigg Town      | 32 | 51  |
| 9.  | Ossett Albion   | 31 | 49  |
| 10. | Kidsgrove Ath   | 34 | 47  |

## 26 March: Away to Brigg Town

I've written this many times before this season; this was going to be a long way to go to lose, but then we don't lose anymore. The supporters' bus was packed, optimism was high and we're going up, via the play-offs that is, but just a few were starting to say it would be automatic promotion. I sat and listened to them doing their sums. Adding up the results from matches we haven't played yet, three points from a win here, a draw from there, definitely got to get a win there and lo-and-behold we were in second place. Anybody would think the people on this bus were biased. But I wonder how many of them nodded in agreement at the criticisms chanted last autumn?

Cold drizzle drifted across the ground as a grey lifeless sky hung low over the ground. The weather was slightly more interesting then the first half right up to the 43rd minute when Roy Jordan hit a cross from Pat Shaughnessy: 1-0. Suddenly the first 45 minutes had been a delightful display of football, slowly building up to a fantastic goal; well it was for the Telford supporters. Three minutes added time was announced moments later, six minutes later we were still playing. Bernard was bellowing across the pitch at the referee, urging him to blow the whistle.

The second half was a display of great football; the back row from both sides forgot how to defend as shot followed shot at either end. The crowd 'ooooed' and 'ahhhed' so much it sounded like a pantomime. It was always going to happen, and then it did. They scored to make it 1-1, and 10 minutes later they did it again, 2-1. We couldn't lose could we? But now they were on top and we were on the back foot. We pushed forward, but slowly heads were dropping, passes weren't as accurate; tackles not as fierce. Glenn managed a good ball through to Damien only to see him felled like a tree in the area. Penalty? The ref didn't see it, play on, this was not going to be our day. Our followers were silent. A free kick 30 yards out raised little interest. Jack hit it hard and low, the wall jumped, the ball went through like a 10-pin bowling ball, their 'keeper didn't move, 2-2. Twice after that Alfie could have won it but good goalkeeping stopped him twice. They could have won, but great stops from Stuart kept us in the game.

Then there was a slight problem; if the football in the second half had been anything but flat, the tyres on the bus were the opposite. To be accurate the tyres on the team bus, the supporters' bus and the minibus were all flat on the bottom, it was only the bottom bit but it does stop them from going round. If that happens when they draw, I'm almost glad we didn't win.

The team bus was quiet on the way home. Last week Bernard told me good teams go away from home, play badly and win 1-0. Well this week a good team went a long way from home and drew 2-2. It's a dream to think we can keep this run up, but let's enjoy it while it lasts.

Unibond Northern League Division One 28 March 2005
(Top 10)

|     |               | P  | Pts |
| --- | ------------- | -- | --- |
| 1.  | North Ferriby | 35 | 67  |
| 2.  | Willenhall Town | 33 | 67 |
| 3.  | Ilkeston Town | 33 | 65  |
| **4.** | **AFC Telford U** | **35** | **63** |
| 5.  | Kendal Town   | 34 | 58  |
| 6.  | Gresley Rovers | 34 | 55 |
| 7.  | Eastwood Town | 35 | 53  |
| 8.  | Ossett Albion | 33 | 52  |
| 9.  | Brigg Town    | 33 | 52  |
| 10. | Kidsgrove Ath | 35 | 48  |

## 29 March: Home to Willenhall Town

There are times words cannot express the emotion this game can cause. Exactly 14 days ago I travelled home from Woodley with a feeling of elation - which goal do I choose as my favourite? Which moment will live on in my mind forever? A clinical demolition, a majestic hat-trick, a night to remember.

Then tonight it was 2-1 with 10 seconds to go; were they offside, was the time up? The only thing I am sure of is that tonight will also live on for ever and be debated long into the night for many years to come 2-2.

Above: Roy Jordan celebrates his goal against Woodley Sports.

Right: Telford defender Duane Courtney beats Mossley forward Rhodri Giggs, brother of Manchester United's Ryan, to the ball.

# 10. April

## 2 April: Away to Warrington Town

The only thing I knew about Warrington before today was that the IRA once planted a bomb there and killed a teenage boy, so whatever happened today I will know of the place for a more positive reason. But you really couldn't make this stuff up. As we walked across the car park at Warrington one of their stewards directed us to the turnstiles: "The main gate's locked," he said. Derek looked at his truck stacked high with gear and laughed. "Sorry mate," the man went on "we can't find the key to the big gate." A 12-year-old on a mountain bike then bounced up the kerb shouting and waving a single key. "Looks like you're in," the man added. Well he was nearly right, it was the key to the side gate so we unloaded the truck, carried the gear and bags in, then loaded the truck again.

It's quite ironic really that we were playing Warrington today after what happened against Willenhall Town on Tuesday. Last October we had a final minute goal disallowed against them. So today would we get revenge for a last minute goal that should have stood or would we let the memory of a Willenhall's last minute goal beat us again?

Today was going to be the true test of a manager, to pick his men up, remind them of their unbeaten run and push for the automatic promotion places even though the teams ahead of us have games in hand. A win today and we are still in with a chance, a defeat and everything could be over. Everyone is confident we can win but we do seem to have the knack of making life hard for ourselves.

The opening moments made it clear. We began where we left off last October - battering them. Duane headed in at about 10 minutes from a great in-swinging corner from Sean, 1-0. Just on the half hour, Jack jumped to head in another, the ground vibrated as he landed and more of him wobbled than should have, but no one cared, 2-0. Moments before half-time Neil ran onto what was about our 10th corner and hit it hard into the net: 3-0. Days like this don't happen very often. Sean managed to get himself concussed just before the break and young Tom Griffin came on.

There must have been a Warrington supporter there somewhere but if there was I couldn't hear them. Their programme seller complained that we had brought too many supporters with us and he couldn't keep up with the demand. I just thought they should have printed more programmes or am I being awkward? Every team we have played has had their biggest gate against us and had a good pay day.

Round two and we put two more past them; this was getting boring, 5-0. Are we building ourselves up for a fall, can we keep this up? Can we get automatic promotion? Did that last minute goal from Willenhall really make that an unattainable dream? Did we lose too many last autumn?

Roy Jordan scores a wonder goal on the volley at Warrington Town
as Telford win 5-0.

Telford fans celebrate the team's goal at Rossendale.

There are 15 points left to play for. Can we really go the rest of the season without losing? Surely an impossible dream, but as imperfect as it might be there is relative peace in Northern Ireland right now and a decade ago when they were killing teenage boys in Warrington, that was also an impossible dream.

## 9 April: Away to Ossett Albion

Take the M1 to junction 40 and follow the A638 to Ossett and that's really all there is to the place. A man from Ossett once wrote a book that was turned into a film that had 'Alf Roberts' from *Coronation Street* in it, and after an extensive five minute search of the internet was about the most exciting thing I could find about the place. But would it be the setting for our 16th game without defeat. Yes I know we lost in the Chairman's Cup, but that was so long ago now, who cares, and tell me who won it anyway.

It was a cold blustery day, the bus rocked with the cross-wind as we arrived at the ground. The video had played all the way up the motorway with no one really watching it and the never ending game of cards had continued, but more quietly than normal. Everyone seems subdued; it seems that this unbeaten record is more of a weight than many might think. Earlier this season Arsenal had gone finished their unbeaten run of 49 games, but lost three of the next six after losing to Manchester United. Nothing but promotion will now be good enough and these men, now sat quietly at the back of the bus know that.

By 2.50pm the wind was up to what seemed like gale-force and a black sky was building in the distance. At kick off Bernard made his intentions clear, a pass to Big Jack and a shot from the halfway line with the second touch of the match. Sean hit the post minutes later and Duane was a rock at the back. We were showing class and confidence. You could tell it was going to happen and at about the half-hour Glenn made a long cross into the box for Kyle to score with his head, 1-0. Six months ago you could tell it was going to happen, but then it wasn't Telford that were doing the scoring.

Then it happened like it always does. It is an old saying that there are three people on any football pitch who aren't allowed to make a mistake: the referee and two goalkeepers. They cleared long and Stuart hesitated for a moment before coming to meet it, their man ran onto the kick and almost looked embarrassed as he scored. Everyone that ground felt for Stuart, a figure so immense in goal, so committed to his cause, this unbeaten run would not be there without him: there can only be one position more lonely that being in goal, that is being in goal just after a mistake, 1-1.

We came back and battered them. Roy hit a screamer high and wide, but then he can't do anything gently. Damien ran at them and tapped it

Glenn Tolley on the ball as Telford beat Ossett Albion 2-1.

wide, but then he doesn't walk anywhere. Kyle missed a sitter, but he just does that sometimes. Our team would have folded last autumn and settled for a draw only to lose to a last minute goal, but not any more. Just past the hour Damien hit a great cross, and Kyle headed his second to make it 2-1.

With 90 minutes gone a fine drizzle was falling and the wind was very cold. A confused mutter went around the ground like a Mexican wave, "How much longer?" when the tannoy crackled and a broad Yorkshire accent announced "90 minutes 'av now bin played and I'll tell thee more when the ref tells me."

One minute later and it was all over, Ossett were great hosts and fed us stew and Yorkshire pudding after the game. We were now 16 games unbeaten and the expectations are getting higher and the weight of expectation is getting heaver.

Unibond Northern League Division One 9 April 2005
(Top 10)

|  |  | P | Pts |
|---|---|---|---|
| 1. | North Ferriby | 38 | 74 |
| 2. | Willenhall Town | 37 | 73 |
| **3.** | **AFC Telford U** | **38** | **70** |
| 4. | Ilkeston Town | 36 | 69 |
| 5. | Kendal Town | 38 | 65 |
| 6. | Eastwood Town | 38 | 60 |
| 7. | Gresley Rovers | 37 | 59 |
| 8. | Mossley | 36 | 57 |
| 9. | Brigg Town | 37 | 55 |
| 10. | Ossett Albion | 37 | 54 |

## 11 April

The weekend results showed that nothing was decided. We're third, four points behind North Ferriby, but Ilkeston were in fourth place only one point behind with two games in hand, the old enemy Willenhall stayed stubbornly in second with three points and a game in hand on us. There were still four games and a long way to go.

## 12 April: Home to Belper Town

A 4-0 triumph tonight makes 17 games unbeaten. The play-offs are secure and possibility automatic promotion beckons. Oh where are you now all now the doubters of early season? Where are you now Mr Steve Bleasby? "...It is imperative we get out of this league, this season and McNally has demonstrated he is not capable of doing this and needs to go now while we still have a chance..."

Do you come to the Bucks Head in disguise? You shouldn't - at least you were brave enough to put your thoughts in writing. I'll bet there was not one person in the ground tonight who beat the roof of our dugout at Rocester or chanted "What a load of rubbish" from the safety of the dark at Kidsgrove, that cold damp night last October.

But the season is not over yet, there are three games to go and nothing is yet secure.

## 13 April

I logged on to the league website; as I left the ground last night I had heard a rumour about Willenhall. It's true: they drew 1-1 with Shepshed.

Unibond Northern League Division One 13 April 2005
(Top 10)

|     |                | P  | Pts |
| --- | -------------- | -- | --- |
| 1.  | North Ferriby  | 39 | 77  |
| 2.  | Willenhall Town | 38 | 74  |
| **3.**  | **AFC Telford U** | **39** | **73**  |
| 4.  | Ilkeston Town  | 37 | 70  |
| 5.  | Kendal Town    | 38 | 65  |
| 6.  | Eastwood Town  | 39 | 63  |
| 7.  | Mossley        | 37 | 60  |
| 8.  | Gresley Rovers | 38 | 59  |
| 9.  | Brigg Town     | 38 | 56  |
| 10. | Ossett Albion  | 38 | 54  |

## 14 April

Ilkeston Town 2 Brigg Town 2; Oh Brigg we love you.

## 16 April: Home to Mossley

My two main memories of today are of noise and a feeling of foreboding. A wall of noise rolled from the Hutchinson Stand so loud I felt like I could touch it, as a drum beat out an uneven rhythm. But for all the noise, and drums and air-horns I couldn't get way from that feeling that this all seems too good to be true: a 5-0 and a 4-0 in the last three matches, 18 games unbeaten, other teams in the League doing us favours; I just kept getting that feeling that we were heading for an almighty fall. The whole thing seemed like a dream. What odds you could have got on this before Christmas? The team, who went all the way to Kendal to lose like amateurs last October, who got stuffed by Stocksbridge last September, now second in the League with three games to go.

We came out fighting and in under five minutes Glenn centred into the box for Kyle to head against the crossbar but that was about it. We just didn't seem to get going and the foreboding I had before the match seemed justified. The noise had started to fade and that's always a bad sign. Damien got the volume up a bit with a hard shot, but you just knew it was going to be saved. The body language of the crowd said it, you could hear it - or not - in the shouts of the crowd, we were not playing well; was today to be the day that the wheels came off? We all knew it couldn't last.

The second half came and within minutes they were through. Only the post stopped a certain goal. Even the drum had been silenced by now, we had to win, the teams around us still had games in hand and a draw would not do. That win against Belper suddenly seemed a long way away. Then Sean hit a corner and Duane rose with the grace of a ballet dancer to head home, 1-0. The drum was beating loudly, but they came back. Nothing was decided yet. We held our breath, Darren chased down the wing, but ended up in the corner, this wasn't to be a day for 4-0, but he stayed on his feet to hit a cross to the box, Kyle turned it to Glenn who hit it hard and a better goal will never be scored, 2-0. The drum was beating, we were singing.

18 games unbeaten, two games left. Automatic promotion, I don't know. But the dream is still alive.

## 17 April

I looked up the results: Ilkeston Town 0 Warrington 0; Willenhall Town 0 Chorley 3. Yes there is a god, who needs the play-offs; we're going up.

## 19 April

Ilkeston beat Mossley 2-1, but we can still do it.

Unibond Northern League Division One 19 April 2005

|     |                 | P   | Pts |
| --- | --------------- | --- | --- |
| 1.  | North Ferriby   | 40  | 77  |
| **2.** | **AFC Telford U** | **40** | **76** |
| 3.  | Willenhall Town | 39  | 74  |
| 4.  | Ilkeston Town   | 39  | 74  |
| 5.  | Kendal Town     | 39  | 68  |
| 6.  | Eastwood Town   | 40  | 66  |
| 7.  | Gresley Rovers  | 39  | 62  |
| 8.  | Mossley         | 39  | 60  |
| 9.  | Brigg Town      | 40  | 60  |
| 10. | Ossett Albion   | 39  | 57  |

## 23 April: Away to Rossendale United

Bernard said it was just another match, but it could never have been just that. With over 100 of the faithful at the ground for a photo before we left, there was always that feeling that today would be an eventful day. The journey there was quick with no traffic jams, no tours of the town, no

95

players getting lost; it had only taken the entire season to get the travelling right. We did manage a slight detour, coming home we had to go back to the ground; we'd left one of the directors behind but I promised Dave Topping I wouldn't mention it.

On August bank holiday last year we managed – just - a 1-1 draw against Rosendale after they obligingly missed a penalty and Alfie scored one. To say it wasn't pretty would be an understatement. Today had to be better. A win and we would have been on for automatic promotion a defeat and it was the play-offs for sure, a draw would just pile on the agony.

An own goal within 10 minutes gave us the lead and an equaliser within 15 gave us the final score. I had a feeling when we played Mossley we were slipping and today I was getting it again, our form had peaked. That was obvious, but would we still be good enough to last the season out? Would Ilkeston or Willenhall do us a favour? We needed one; on the pitch it wasn't looking good. Would this incredible unbeaten run come to an end in the next 45 minutes?

Then it got worse, the second half had only just begun when it happened. The whistle had blown, play was stopping, as the ball came into the edge of our box, their striker ran onto it, Stuart came the other way, it looked like nothing but it was something. Stuart lay there and clutched his leg. Bernard stood and stared, 900 of us stood in silence; I watched Rudi's hands, they seemed to go into slow motion as they rotated to say change. This could not get worse, we were playing badly and now we had no keeper.

St George's Day is a day for heroes. Darren went in goal, but did not look comfortable. They tried to test him, their striker ran through him as he kicked to clear, now we were all silent again as he limped back to his line. To lose one goalkeeper is unfortunate, but two, well that's down right careless.

They came again, Darren punched away, then they shot wide, they came again, he dived to block but didn't hold, Neil kicked for a corner, we cleared and kicked long. People were looking away, Lee was silent. The ref was collecting names like an autograph hunter. It was just a pity he did it before Stuart was injured. Bernard went for bust as he sent Neil up the field, we had eight men in their box and corner after corner but still we couldn't score. And that was it 1-1, one injured goalkeeper and one match to play.

And a sad footnote to the day: Rossendale had a good looking female physio. The language and behaviour of a few fans towards her was an embarrassment to us all. Later two men were thrown off the supporters' bus for drunken and stupid behaviour. Neither I nor anyone I know condoned this conduct.

## 24 April

It's Sunday, but I was out of the house at 8.00am. Trying to buy a copy of the *Sunday Mercury*, I knew it had all of the league matches and results in it. I couldn't wait for the website to be updated. Willenhall had lost 2-1 to Chorley and Ilkeston had drawn 1-1 with Gresley. We could still get automatic promotion. Sunday mornings don't start any better than this.

Unibond Northern League Division One 28 April 2005

|     |                | P   | Pts |
| --- | -------------- | --- | --- |
| 1.  | North Ferriby  | 41  | 80  |
| 2.  | Ilkeston Town  | 41  | 78  |
| 3.  | **AFC Telford U** | **41** | **77** |
| 4.  | Willenhall Town | 41 | 77  |
| 5.  | Eastwood Town  | 41  | 69  |
| 6.  | Kendal Town    | 41  | 68  |
| 7.  | Mossley        | 41  | 66  |
| 8.  | Brigg Town     | 41  | 63  |
| 9.  | Gresley Rovers | 41  | 63  |
| 10. | Ossett Albion  | 41  | 58  |

## 30 April: Home to Gresley Rovers

And so it was the last match, the last 90 minutes of the season proper. We had to win and others had to lose, but then we've had to win every match since Christmas. Next Thursday there will be a general election, people were saying it is the longest election campaign they could remember. Well this was the longest end-of-season I think that any team has ever had and at heart we knew it would not be over today, but then it just might be.

The promotion set-up is: first and second go up automatically. In the play-offs: third plays sixth and fourth plays fifth, the highest placed team at home ground. The two winners play of for the third promotion slot at the ground of the highest placed team. We will be promoted if;
- We win and North Ferriby lose;
- We win and Ilkeston lose or draw;
- We draw and Ilkeston lose and Willenhall lose or draw.

Bright sun lit up the Bucks Head in an optimistic way as the team warmed up, each time they ran towards the stand the crowd clapped and they clapped back. There can be no doubt of the dreams they carry on their shoulders, Steve Taylor stood tall and blond on the end of the row, who would be have been him right then. The noise was building, the drum was beating again, but the choir only seemed to know one song "We're going up, we're going up, the Bucks are going up."

97

And then we were off and two minutes later we had the start you couldn't plan. A long throw from Duane hit hard by Sean but blocked, the deflection fell to Damien who did not need a second invitation, the net ballooned and Bernard was in the centre of the pitch, 1-0. A rumour went around Ilkeston were winning but so were we. The pace was frenetic. Steve made a good stop, but still hadn't been tested as he kicked long and hard down the field. His kick was impressive but still doubts lingered in 3,704 minds.

Duane was having the match of his life, the way he battled, the skill he was showing was silencing even the faithful. When a long ball came back it bounced between him and Steve; each seemed to think the other had it when their striker ran through and tapped it home, 1-1. This could not be the end, there was still an hour to go, but for a moment it felt like it was. Gresley rallied and came forward *en masse*, it was the best thing they could have done. Steve made stop after stop, the memory of the goal was gone and he had proved himself, he was not a dodgy keeper.

Ten minutes later Kyle was down, not unusually for him but we had a free kick, it came back off the post as Damien ran in for his second, 2-1. If this had been the Millennium Stadium with the roof closed it would have come off with the noise that went up at that moment. Passion was high, suddenly Sean is down, then he's up and chest-to-chest with one of their players. Bernard looked away, the ref got between them, play started again and we all breathed again.

I was looking at my note pad when the cheer went up, I can't believe I missed the goal of the season, they tell me, Neil hit it hard from 30 yards out and that it flew straighter that a satellite guided missile into the net, 3-1. After the game I was told it was 40 yards, that night I heard 50 yards. Soon he will have scored from the bar in the Whitehouse Hotel while drinking a gin and tonic. But those kind of stories are what days like this are about.

A weird silence hung over the ground for the rest of the game, the football deteriorated, we'd done all we could, they had a goal disallowed and that was all from the last 30 minutes. Then a whisper went around Mossley had equalised against Ferriby and for a few surreal moment the words "Come of Mossley" rolled around the Bucks Head but we knew it wouldn't last. With 10 minutes to go a brief reprisal of "We're going up" came from one corner but it was just optimism, no one had scored. And then it was over we stood in silence waiting for the all knowing score board to tell us what we already knew. The teams around us had not done us the favours we needed, it was the play-offs, we stared at the board and then left in silence; it was as if we had lost.

Duane Courtney, Glenn Tolley and Dean Craven watch on as Damien Charie celebrates his goal against Gresley Rovers at the Bucks Head.

The Telford team celebrate Neil Howarth's extraordinary long-range goal against Gresley Rovers.

## UniBond Northern League First Division final table

| | | P | W | D | L | F | A | GD | Pts |
|---|---|---|---|---|---|---|---|---|---|
| 1 | North Ferriby Utd | 42 | 25 | 8 | 9 | 83 | 49 | 34 | 83 |
| 2 | Ilkeston Town | 42 | 24 | 9 | 9 | 64 | 40 | 24 | 81 |
| **3** | **AFC Telford Utd** | **42** | **23** | **11** | **8** | **78** | **44** | **34** | **80** |
| 4 | Willenhall Town | 42 | 22 | 12 | 8 | 71 | 46 | 25 | 78 |
| 5 | Kendal Town | 42 | 21 | 8 | 13 | 89 | 69 | 20 | 71 |
| 6 | Eastwood Town | 42 | 20 | 9 | 13 | 73 | 54 | 19 | 69 |
| 7 | Mossley | 42 | 20 | 6 | 16 | 81 | 56 | 25 | 66 |
| 8 | Brigg Town | 42 | 15 | 19 | 8 | 59 | 46 | 13 | 64 |
| 9 | Gresley Rovers | 42 | 17 | 12 | 13 | 57 | 53 | 4 | 63 |
| 10 | Kidsgrove Ath | 42 | 15 | 15 | 12 | 60 | 55 | 5 | 60 |
| 11 | Woodley Sports | 42 | 16 | 11 | 15 | 68 | 74 | -6 | 59 |
| 12 | Ossett Albion | 42 | 15 | 13 | 14 | 83 | 74 | 9 | 58 |
| 13 | Colwyn Bay | 42 | 14 | 13 | 15 | 54 | 62 | -8 | 55 |
| 14 | Stocksbridge Park Steels* | 42 | 15 | 9 | 18 | 58 | 58 | 0 | 51 |
| 15 | Shepshed Dynamo | 42 | 13 | 11 | 18 | 53 | 75 | -22 | 50 |
| 16 | Chorley | 42 | 13 | 9 | 20 | 62 | 69 | -7 | 48 |
| 17 | Belper Town | 42 | 13 | 8 | 21 | 57 | 66 | -9 | 47 |
| 18 | Spalding United | 42 | 13 | 8 | 21 | 57 | 69 | -12 | 47 |
| 19 | Clitheroe | 42 | 12 | 10 | 20 | 47 | 57 | -10 | 46 |
| 20 | Warrington Town | 42 | 11 | 13 | 18 | 45 | 59 | -14 | 46 |
| 21 | Rossendale Utd | 42 | 10 | 10 | 22 | 64 | 87 | -23 | 40 |
| 22 | Rocester | 42 | 0 | 6 | 36 | 31 | 132 | -101 | 6 |

*Stocksbridge PS 3 points deducted for breach of rule

# TEAM SHEET
## 2nd May 2005

| | AFC Telford United | | V | | Eastwood Town | |
|---|---|---|---|---|---|---|
| 1 | Steve Taylor | | | 1 | Danny Bryant | |
| 2 | David Andrewartha | | | 2 | Chris Shaw | |
| 3 | Dean Craven | | | 3 | James Whitehead | |
| 4 | Duane Courtney | | | 4 | Lee Soad | |
| 5 | Neil Howarth | | | 5 | Matt Millner | |
| 6 | Jack Cudworth | | | 6 | Paul Gould (C) | |
| 7 | Sean Parrish (c) | | | 7 | Mark Fisher | |
| 8 | Glenn Tolley | | | 8 | Deon Meikle | |
| 9 | Kyle Perry | | | 9 | Peter Knox | |
| 10 | Damien Charie | | | 10 | Gary Sucharewycz | |
| 11 | Roy Jordan | | | 11 | Paul Mitchell | |
| | | | | | | |
| 12 | Alfie Carter | | | 12 | Lindon Meikle | |
| 14 | Leon Drysdale | | | 14 | Adie Francis | |
| 15 | Luke McNally | | | 15 | Kelvin Mushambe | |

| Referee: |
|---|
| C Grundy |
| Fourth Official: |
| A J Martin |

| Assistant: |
|---|
| M Birley |
| Assistant: |
| S J Rushton |

CONSULTING.TECHNOLOGY.OUTSOURCING

The team sheet from the play-off semi-final.
(Courtesy AFC Telford United)

102

# 11. May

## 2 May: Home to Eastwood Town - Play-offs semi-final

Rumour had it that this was going to be easy, rumour had it they would roll over. I wasn't so confident; we hadn't played our best football for a few games now, Eastwood had a back door to promotion. They had nothing to lose, we had everything. And so 48 hours after beating Gresley we were ready to kick off again. Lee sat in the director's box and looked pensive; Bernard stood by the dugout and looked relaxed.

Then God had his say as rain so heavy came down that for a moment the game was in doubt. It seemed fitting somehow after all the training in the rain behind Wrekin College last summer. An inch of water lay on the pitch and the goalmouths looked like mud baths. When the teams came out to warm up the ball left a wave like a boat through water.

Then it was 3.00pm and the waiting was over, three minutes into the game Neil made a save with his hand that any goalkeeper would have been proud of and the ref waved play on. Perhaps luck would be with us today. Eastwood were making life difficult and were up for it. We were the better side, that was obvious, but we had been the better side so many times in the early season and lost, except that this wasn't early season, this was winner-take-all. The crowd was loud, but it was a tense noise easily silenced. If you could bottle nervousness today you could have opened a brewery.

Then they spilt us, and scored, the linesman flagged, offside. We all breathed again. We were not playing well. Slowly the ground fell into silence the lone drum gradually faded as we shifted on our seats or shuffled from one foot to another. We attacked and attacked again, but each foray came to nothing. Big Jack lined up a free kick, he hit it hard and low, the net waved, the ball was in, and the whistle blew, no goal. Then as half-time approached Kyle had a chance but the clearance fell to Glenn, he hit it badly, the ball bounced and bounced again. A moment later it was in. For a second no one was certain, then we were, 1-0.

We spent the second half missing sitters as we seemed to decide that one goal was enough. With five minutes to go Alfie came on for Damien, he ran the ball into the corners time and time again. Slowly we burnt up precious minutes. Memories of Willenhall and lessons learnt the hard way came flooding back as a thousand whistles came from the crowd. And then it was over: 1-0 but still nothing was decided.

Kendal Town had won 1-0 at Willenhall, and would come to the Bucks' Head on Saturday to decide the third promotion place.

Telford defender Jack Cudworth makes a last ditch tackle to win the ball against Eastwood Town.

Damien Charie celebrates Glenn Tolley's goal.

Bernard McNally and physio Brin May encourage the players from the sidelines against Eastwood Town.

Roy Jordan in action against Eastwood Town.

Bernard McNally salutes the Telford fans after the play-off victory against Eastwood Town.

## 7 May: Home to Kendal Town - Play-off final

And so this was it, sudden death, the 20 games unbeaten counted for nothing, the 4-0 at Woodley, the 5-0 at Warrington counted for nothing, third in the league and 80 points on the board counted for nothing.

The Bucks Head had seen so many moods this season, but nothing could compare to the emotion that filled its walls today. Clichéd descriptions of flags and shirts could not convey the landscape of colour and hope that cascaded from the terraces like water over Niagara Falls.

Then it was over, 2-1. We won, we were up, it was over. And the club that less than a year ago had one mobile phone and no credit, one whistle and a bag of new balls, a new manager and no players had won promotion the hard way.

Those who were there today could never explain the feeling and those who were not would never understand anyway.

If this book had not been a diary any reader would have said it was too much of a fairytale to be true. Too much of a dramatic ending to have really happened, but it did and I feel privileged to have been there to record it.

The achievements of this season are proof that football is about more than money, more than business. AFC Telford United is proof that there is such a thing as society, that groups of people working together for a common cause for no other reason than belief are more powerful than any venture capitalist. The volunteers with the brooms sweeping up after every home game are proof of it, the directors who have changed their lives are proof of it, the men and women clutching armfuls of programmes are proof of it.

And the journey that had taken us from the rain of Eastwood to the despair of Kidsgrove, through the mud of Stocksbridge, to the joy of Woodley, the disbelief at Willenhall, the pain of Rossendale was over; But answer me honestly would those of you who were there changed one minute of it? I know I wouldn't.

Roy Jordan fires in the equaliser for Telford against Kendal Town...

... and runs away to celebrate the goal that levelled the scores at 1-1.

Neil Howarth jumps high to challenge the Kendal Town goalkeeper.

Sean Parrish celebrates scoring the winning goal that promoted AFC Telford United to the Unibond League Premier Division.

Duane Courtney leads the celebrations with the Telford players.

AFC Telford United fans celebrate their team's victory against Kendal Town.

The two goalscorers, Roy Jordan and Sean Parrish stand side by side and lead the Telford players in celebrating their victory.

Telford fans celebrate their team's victory against Kendal Town.

# Appendix 1: The players

In its first season AFC Telford fielded 35 players, some once, some twice, and some in almost every match. A bit like characters in a film - you have the stars and the supporting cast.

AFC Telford United: The stars 2004-05 - in no particular order

### Stuart Brock
*Position: Goalkeeper*
Stuart is the tall quiet menacing type. He prefers to play with at least half an inch of stubble on his face, always quiet with a smile or a frown. Hands like shovels and a competitive edge like a razor blade; the only member of the team Sean seems wary of. His own biggest critic and a solid pro whom it's difficult not to like. Made over 230 league appearances for Kidderminster Harriers, including winning the Conference title.

### David Andrewartha
*Position: Defender*
David is quiet and seems a bit shy; a spotless, clean appearance, smart clothes and a friendly smile (when he's not playing). Prefers to stay out of mischief and card games on the team bus. David is usually seen wearing earphones and listening to music. When playing he's utterly committed and tougher than he looks. Played for Aston Villa youth team and Ludlow Town.

### Leon Drysdale
*Position: Midfield*
Leon is definitely not tall or quiet; difficult to tie down, someone you'd want with you if your back was against the wall. Beckham-like free kicks and often found at the root of mischief on the team coach. Plays and parties with equal skill, the kind of lad I would have liked to be mates with at school. Made 52+14 league appearances for Shrewsbury Town between 1998 and 2004.

### Neil Howarth
*Position: Defender*
Neil is far too tall and a really nice guy; doesn't seem to do very much but we win when he plays and lose when he doesn't. Assistant coach, bright and good with words - could easily be a sportswriter one day. Over 400 league appearances, previous clubs include Burnley, Cheltenham and Macclesfield. Captained the latter in the 1996 FA Trophy final at Wembley.

### Jack Cudworth
*Position: Defender*
Big Jack to his friends and it's not because he is tall. Takes great free kicks, but not bent around the wall with precision; they go through the wall with power taking body parts with them. One of the bravest players I have ever seen, not a subtle footballer, and I doubt he cares. Formerly with West Bromwich Albion and Racing Club Warwick.

## Sean Parrish
*Position: Midfield*

Sean is the nosiest player anyone will ever see or hear. Captain and takes the job seriously, constantly driving the team on and leads by example. When not playing cards or reading the *Racing Post,* he could usually be found two inches from the ref putting forward the team's case. This was his second spell at Telford, 250 league appearances, previous clubs include Kidderminster Harriers and Northampton Town. Played at Wembley for Northampton in play-off final.

## Luke McNally
*Position: Midfield*

The boss's son and in the team completely on merit; fit intelligent and tougher than he looks. Luke was once on the books of Birmingham City but you can't hold that against him forever. Former clubs include Rushall Olympic.

## Kyle Perry
*Position: Striker*

Kyle is a big lad who scores goals and falls over at about the same rate. A talented artist, quiet and a good footballer. Always smiling, sensitive (yes, a sensitive footballer) and not bad looking either, in fact there is nothing to be rude about. Signed on loan from Walsall.

## Damien Charie
*Position: Forward*

Damien is tall and very blond, looks like Rod Stewart but I can't comment on his singing voice. He never stops running and seems to do everything at speed. Formerly with Hednesford Town.

## Duane Courtney
*Position: Defender*

Duane is tall and far too good looking to stand next to me. Quiet and intelligent he usually manages to avoid Leon's mischief but occasionally gets drawn in. Modest, he gives little away but there's a lot more going on between his ears than he lets on. Formerly with Birmingham City.

## Alfie Carter
*Position: Forward*

Tall, cool, fast, good looking and the most infuriating player in the squad. You can't help but like him. Just as you decide he should be sacked he does something fantastic. Just as you call him idle he runs himself into the ground. Can always be found on the back seat of the bus and is usually up to no-good there. Previous clubs include Gillingham and Walsall.

## Glenn Tolley
*Position: Defender*

A nice lad and constantly improving; released by Shrewsbury Town, his self-confidence was down in August. Applied himself like a pro and worked his way to the side with hard work. Quiet, polite and honest. Previously played for Northich Victoria, won under-20 cap for Wales.

### Roy Jordan
*Position: Defender*
Roy can't do anything gently, the only player to make Big Jack look delicate. Never scores consolation goals and they are never side-footed over the line in a laid-back way. Previously played for Westfields.

### Dean Craven
*Position: Defender*
The most popular member of the squad; never quite scored but if he had the roof would have come off. Short and quick like a shaken bottle of pop; no one could put more energy into a game. Usually found losing at cards or having the mickey taken out of him by Sean. Always takes life in his stride, a thoroughly nice guy. Previous clubs include Shrewsbury Town, Hereford United and Hednesford Town.

### Darren Alexander
*Position: Striker and once a goalkeeper*
I didn't get to know him that well. Not a natural goalie but brave and solid. On a day when we needed heroes he was one.

### Steve Taylor
*Position: Goalkeeper*
Tall and blond, we only saw him in the last three matches, but I think he became a hero to a lot of people. To come in and play the last league match and the two play-offs to an audience of over 3,000 says it all about his character. Previously with Market Drayton Town, also played cricket for Warwickshire CCC.

### The supporting cast
David Arrowsmith, Tom Barnet, Mark Briggs, Tom Griffin, Gareth Jennings, Mathew Johnson, Andreas Kattos, Jordan King, Arron Lloyd, Paul Moore, Sean Platt, Andy Pryce, Dion Scott, Pat Shaughnessy, Ian Simms, Ally Smith, Nick Smith, Carl Tranter, Ben Willletts.

# Appendix 2: Statistics and records

## Player appearances

| | | League | | Cups | | Total | |
|---|---|---|---|---|---|---|---|
| | | App | G | App | G | App | G |
| 1. | Darren Alexander | 3+4 | 2 | 0 | 0 | 3+4 | 2 |
| 2. | David Andrewartha | 25+3 | 1 | 3 | 0 | 28+3 | 1 |
| 3. | David Arrowsmith | 3 | 0 | 0 | 0 | 3 | 0 |
| 4. | Tom Barnett | 0+1 | 0 | 0 | 0 | 0+1 | 0 |
| 5. | Mark Briggs | 5 | 0 | 1 | 0 | 6 | 0 |
| 6. | Stuart Brock | 37 | 0 | 4 | 0 | 41 | 0 |
| 7. | Alfie Carter | 18+16 | 11 | 2+2 | 0 | 20+18 | 11 |
| 8. | Duane Courtney | 42 | 2 | 5 | 1 | 47 | 3 |
| 9. | Damien Charie | 18+9 | 7 | 2 | 2 | 20+9 | 9 |
| 10. | Dean Craven | 31+3 | 0 | 1 | 0 | 32+3 | 0 |
| 11. | Jack Cudworth | 24 | 5 | 2 | 0 | 26 | 5 |
| 12. | Leon Drysdale | 16+4 | 5 | 3 | 0 | 19+4 | 5 |
| 13. | Tom Griffin | 4+3 | 0 | 2 | 0 | 6+3 | 0 |
| 14. | Neil Howarth | 39 | 3 | 4 | 1 | 43 | 4 |
| 15. | Gareth Jennings | 4+3 | 0 | 1+2 | 0 | 5+5 | 0 |
| 16. | Mathew Johnson | 11+4 | 0 | 2 | 0 | 13+4 | 0 |
| 17. | Roy Jordan | 19+1 | 4 | 2 | 0 | 21+1 | 4 |
| 18. | Andreas Kattos | 7+4 | 1 | 2 | 0 | 9+4 | 1 |
| 19. | Jordan King | 1+1 | 0 | 0 | 0 | 1+1 | 0 |
| 20. | Arron Lloyd | 0+3 | 0 | 1 | 0 | 1+3 | 0 |
| 21. | Luke McNally | 26+1 | 0 | 2+2 | 1 | 28+3 | 1 |
| 22. | Paul Moore | 9+1 | 2 | 0+2 | 0 | 9+3 | 2 |
| 23. | Sean Parrish | 41 | 4 | 4 | 0 | 45 | 4 |
| 24. | Kyle Perry | 31 | 22 | 4 | 1 | 35 | 23 |
| 25. | Sean Platt | 2 | 0 | 0 | 0 | 2 | 0 |
| 26. | Andy Pryce | 1 | 0 | 1 | 0 | 2 | 0 |
| 27. | Dion Scott | 0 | 0 | 0 | 0 | 0 | 0 |
| 28. | Pat Shaughnessy | 2+1 | 0 | 0 | 0 | 2+1 | 0 |
| 29. | Ian Simms | 3 | 0 | 0 | 0 | 3 | 0 |
| 30. | Ally Smith | 2 | 0 | 0 | 0 | 2 | 0 |
| 31. | Nick Smith | 3+1 | 0 | 0 | 0 | 3+1 | 0 |
| 32. | Steve Taylor | 3 | 0 | 0 | 0 | 3 | 0 |
| 33. | Glenn Tolley | 34+3 | 4 | 1 | 0 | 35+3 | 4 |
| 34. | Carl Tranter | 8+8 | 5 | 3+1 | 0 | 11+9 | 5 |
| 35. | Ben Willetts | 2 | 0 | 1 | 0 | 3 | 0 |

(Above excluding friendlies and Staffordshire Senior Cup)

## AFC Telford United results 2004-2005

All league matches unless otherwise stated

**July**

| | | | | |
|---|---|---|---|---|
| Sat 17 | Newtown | A - Fr | 2-2 | (Tranter, Howarth) |
| Thu 22 | Ludlow | A - SSC semi-final | 3-1 | (Willetts, Carter, McKnight) |
| Sat 24 | Bromsgrove | A - Fr | 1-2 | (Carter) |
| Tue 27 | Shrewsbury Town | A - SSC Final | 1-5 | (Carter) |
| Sat 31 | Hednesford | A - Fr | 1-3 | (Carter) |

## August

| | | | | |
|---|---|---|---|---|
| Mon 2 | Hummell Korea | H - Fr | 1-0 (McKnight) (At Shifnal) | |
| Sat 7 | T.N.S A | A - Fr | 1-0 (McNally) | |
| Wed 11 | Market Drayton | A - Fr | 3-0 (McNally 2, Lloyd) | |
| | | | | |
| Sat 21 | North Ferriby Utd | H | 2-2 (Carter 2) | 1,836 |
| Tue 24 | Eastwood Town | A | 0-1 | 348 |
| Sat 28 | Chorley | A | 3-1 (Parrish, Moore, Tranter) | 326 |
| Mon 30 | Rossendale Utd | H | 1-1 (Carter) | 1,618 |

## September

| | | | | |
|---|---|---|---|---|
| Sat 4 | Horden CW | A (FA Cup prel) | 0-1 | 192 |
| Tue 7 | Colwyn Bay | H | 1-0 (Parrish) | 1,352 |
| Sat 11 | Brigg Town | H | 0-2 | 1,470 |
| Tue 14 | Gresley Rovers | A | 2-0 (Perry 2) | 517 |
| Sat 25 | Stocksbridge PS | H | 1-3 (Perry) | 1,460 |
| Tue 28 | Shepshed Dyn | H | 2-0 (Drysdale, Perry) | 1,060 |

## October

| | | | | |
|---|---|---|---|---|
| Sat 2 | Rocester | A | 5-3 (Drysdale, Perry, Tranter 3) | 317 |
| Tue 5 | Warrington Town | H | 1-1 (Tranter) | 1,357 |
| Thur 7 | Kidsgrove Ath | A (FAT prel) | 2-4 (Courtney, Howarth) | 330 |
| Wed 13 | Shepshed Dyn | A | 2-1 (Perry 2) | 219 |
| Sat 16 | Clitheroe | H | 0-2 | 1,426 |
| Tue 19 | Rocester | H | 2-0 (Moore, Tolley) | 1,025 |
| Sat 23 | Kendal Town | A | 2-4 (Kattos, Parrish) | 317 |
| Tue 26 | Willenhall Town | H (ULCC 1) | 1-3 (Perry) | 989 |
| Sat 30 | North Ferriby Utd | A | 0-1 | 261 |

## November

| | | | | |
|---|---|---|---|---|
| Sat 6 | Ilkeston Town | A | 3-2 (Perry 2, Charie) | 538 |
| Sat 13 | Osset Albion | H | 3-3 (Howarth, Perry Charie) | 1,402 |
| Tue 30 | Kidsgrove | H | 0-2 | 1,201 |

## December

| | | | | |
|---|---|---|---|---|
| Sat 4 | Spalding Utd | H | 0-0 | 1,120 |
| Sat 11 | Colwyn Bay | A | 3-0 (Perry 3) | 420 |
| Sat 18 | Spalding Utd | A | 2-1 (Tolley, Cudworth) | 241 |
| Thur 30 | Willenhall Town | A | 0-1 | 905 |

## January

| | | | | |
|---|---|---|---|---|
| Mon 3 | Kendal Town | H | 4-1 (Perry, Drysdale, Carter 2) | 1,442 |
| Sat 8 | Eastwood Town | H | 2-0 (Perry, Charie) | 1,316 |
| Sat 15 | Kidsgrove Ath | A | 2-2 (Charie, Carter) | 479 |
| Sat 22 | Stocksbridge PS | H (CC) | 2-1 (Charie, McNally) | 904 |
| Sat 29 | Belper Town | A | 1-1 (Perry) | 395 |

## February

| | | | | |
|---|---|---|---|---|
| Sat 5 | Ilkeston Town | H | 1-0 (Perry) | 3,740 |
| Sat 12 | Stocksbridge PS | A | 2-1 (Carter 2) | 338 |
| Sat 19 | Woodley Sports | H | 1-0 (Perry) | 1,543 |
| Sat 26 | Clitheroe | A | 1-1 (Cudworth) | 421 |

## March

| | | | | |
|---|---|---|---|---|
| Sat 5 | Kidsgrove Ath | H (CC) | 1-3 (Charie) | 1,110 |
| Sat 12 | Chorley | H | 3-0 (Alexander, Drysdale 2) | 1,352 |
| Tue 15 | Woodley Sports | A | 4-0 (Jordan, Carter 3) | 216 |

| | | | | |
|---|---|---|---|---|
| Sat 19 | Mossley | A | 1-0 (Alexander) | 476 |
| Sat 26 | Brigg Town | A | 2-2 (Jordan, Cudworth) | 368 |
| Tue 29 | Willenhall Town | H | 2-2 (Perry, Parrish) | 2,232 |

**April**

| | | | | |
|---|---|---|---|---|
| Sat 2 | Warrington Town | A | 5-0 (Courtney, Cudworth 2, Howarth, Jordan) | 423 |
| Sat 9 | Osset Albion | A | 2-1 (Perry 2) | 339 |
| Tue 12 | Belper Town | H | 4-0 (Perry, Charie, Andrewartha, Jordan) | 1,641 |
| Sat 16 | Mossley | H | 2-0 (Courtney, Tolley) | 2,014 |
| Sat 23 | Rossendale Utd | A | 1-0 (Carter) | 1,036 |
| Sat 30 | Gresley Rovers | H | 3-1 (Charie 2, Howarth) | 3,774 |

**May**

| | | | | |
|---|---|---|---|---|
| Mon 2 | Eastwood Town | H (PO semi-final) | 1-0 (Tolley) | 2,503 |
| Sat 7 | Kendal Town | H (PO Final) | 2-1 (Jordan, Parrish) | 4,215 |

Fr: Friendly
FAC: FA Cup
FAT: FA Trophy
PO: Play-off
CC: Chairman's Cup
ULCC: Unibond League Challenge Cup
SSC: Staffordshire Senior Cup

119

## Appendix 3: The Unibond Northern League Division One clubs

*AFC Telford United:* Founded in 2004 following collapse of Telford United FC. The 'old' club founded in 1876, played in Conference, FA Trophy winners 3 times.

*Belper Town:* Founded 1883. Won Northern Counties League 1984-85 and Midland Counties League 1979-80.

*Brigg Town:* Founded 1864. Won FA Vase 1995-96.

*Chorley:* Founded 1883, formerly played in Conference. Won Northern Premier League 1987-88.

*Clitheroe:* Founded 1877. FA Vase finalists 1995-96.

*Colwyn Bay:* Founded 1885. Played in Welsh leagues until joined North West Counties League in 1984.

*Eastwood Town:* Founded 1953. Started playing in Notts Alliance until 1961.

*Gresley Rovers:* Founded 1882. FA Vase finalists 1990-91. Previously played in Southern League.

*Ilkeston Town:* Reformed in 1945. Previously in Southern League.

*Kendal Town:* Founded 1920. Formerly in Northern Premier League and North West Counties League.

*Kidsgrove Athletic:* Founded 1952. Won North West Counties League Division 1 in 1996-97.

*Mossley:* Founded 1903. FA Trophy finalists 1979-80.

*North Ferriby United:* Founded 1934. FA Vase finalists 1996-97.

*Ossett Albion:* Founded 1944. Progressed from local leagues.

*Rocester:* Founded 1876. Previously in Southern League.

*Rossendale United:* Founded 1898. Won North West Counties League Division 1 in 1988-89.

*Shepshed Dynamo:* Reformed in 1994, previously played as Shepshed Albion and Shepshed Charterhouse.

*Spalding United:* Founded 1921. Won United Counties League four times. Previously in Southern League.

*Stocksbridge Park Steels:* Founded in 1986 from merger of Stocksbridge Works and Oxley Park.

*Warrington Town:* Founded 1948. FA Vase finalists 1986-87.

*Willenhall Town:* Founded 1953. FA Vase finalists 1980-81. Previously played in Midland Alliance.

*Woodley Sports:* Founded 1970. Based in Stockport.